HOCKEY'S TOP 100

DON WEEKES

and

KERRY BANKS

HOCKEY'S TOP 100

The

GAME'S GREATEST GOALS

GREYSTONE BOOKS

D&M PUBLISHERS INC.

Vancouver/Toronto/Berkeley

To the hockey fan in all of us—D.W.
To Jack and Lulu, my partners in crime—K.B.

Greystone Books
An imprint of D&M Publishers Inc.
2323 Quebec Street, Suite 201
Vancouver BC Canada V5T 4S7
www.greystonebooks.com

Cataloguing in Publication data available
from Library and Archives Canada
ISBN 978-1-55365-660-9 (Canadian edition)
ISBN 978-1-55365-504-6 (US edition)

Editing by Derek Fairbridge
Cover design by Jessica Sullivan
Text design by Heather Pringle
Printed and bound in China by C&C Offset Printing Co., Ltd.
Text printed on acid-free paper
Distributed in the U.S. by Publishers Group West

We gratefully acknowledge the financial support of the Canada Council
for the Arts, the British Columbia Arts Council, the Province of British
Columbia through the Book Publishing Tax Credit and the Government of
Canada through the Canada Book Fund for our publishing activities.

INTRODUCTION

We knew from the drop of the puck that this book meant trouble. Write about hockey's greatest goals and a whole whack of people will disagree with your choices and your rankings. It's guaranteed.

Knowing that achieving consensus is impossible, we chose to present the story of hockey's top 100 goals from our vantage point: with an eye on history and the highlight reel. Faced with an overwhelming selection of game changers, historic firsts, record breakers and championship clinchers to chose from, to say nothing of the many truly beautiful goals that have graced our game, we first had to define what the phrase "great goal" really meant.

Mention "great goal" to most fans and they will instantly think of some recent piece of razzle-dazzle by Rick Nash or Alexander Ovechkin. It's a visual age and the nightly sports highlights and YouTube have pushed this type of goal to the front ranks of many people's consciousness. But this isn't the only type of hockey goal that qualifies as "great." Well, at least, not in our book. The truth is, the stylish goal, while dandy to look at, often doesn't have much staying power, unless it happens to be linked to some larger event. In fact, many of the goals we have ranked highly are not things of beauty. Instead they are great because of what makes them special, which is almost always a great story.

Although we didn't ignore the highlight-reel monsters, we cast a wider net, extending our search for great goals back to before the advent of television. If you are not familiar with such names as Frank Boucher, John Garrison and Mush March, this book will certainly bring their fame to the fore. We didn't limit ourselves to NHL action either—we included great goals plucked from the annals of international hockey, as well. Jaroslav Holik, take a bow.

According to our standards, "great" includes prominent historical goals, those that mark major milestones in the game. Think Maurice Richard. Think Wayne Gretzky. Great also applies to goals that changed hockey in some significant way such as Jean Béliveau's devastating 1955 hat trick, all three goals scored in 44 seconds on the same power play. It changed the man-advantage rule forever. Great can also be used to describe a memorable goal that is scored under extraordinary circumstances, such as Bobby Baun's overtime playoff winner for the Toronto Maple Leafs in the 1964 Stanley Cup Final, a goal that Baun banged home while playing on a busted leg.

Equally deserving are goals that ended epic marathons, such as Modere "Mud" Bruneteau's winner in the sixth overtime period of a 1936 playoff tilt. They didn't have ice-cleaning machines in those days, so we can guess that the condition of the ice must have been brutal. No video exists, but it's a safe bet that Bruneteau's clincher was no work of art.

Of course, there is also the big game goal, the one that is scored in a pressure-charged situation that decides a playoff series or an important game. Think Sidney Crosby. Think Mario Lemieux. Then too, there are goals that assume greatness because they cap amazing comebacks. Think John Tonelli and the New York Islanders' inspiring return from the brink of defeat in the 1982 playoffs. The adjective also applies to those rare iconic goals, the ones that stand out because of who scored them, and how, and what they have come to represent. Think Bobby Orr and you can still see him flying.

Finally, our greatest challenge may have been finding the optimum images. We discovered that some goals either didn't have photos of the play itself, or the goal's photo wasn't very special. In some cases, such as Bobby Hull, Howie Morenz and Jarome Iginla, we chose images that reveal another view of the player and his achievement.

So here it is—hockey's top 100 goals of all time.

Don Weekes, Kerry Banks

"HENDERSON HAS SCORED FOR CANADA!"

Paul Henderson, Canada, September 28, 1972

The pressure mounted as the time ticked down at Moscow's Luzhniki Arena. The game was tied 5–5 and world hockey supremacy hung in the balance. Canada had clawed its way back from a 3–1–1 series deficit, beating the Soviet Union twice on clutch game winners by winger Paul Henderson, but still needed another huge goal to capture the epic 1972 Summit Series. In the dying seconds of play, goalie Vladislav Tretiak kicked out a Phil Esposito shot. The ever-dangerous Henderson pounced on the rebound and the Russian netminder stopped a second shot. Then, while falling, Henderson stabbed at it again, and the puck slipped into the net. As the red light flashed, Foster Hewitt's shrill warble rang out, "Henderson has scored for Canada!" Tretiak lay flat on his back and defenseman Yuri Liapkin stared off in disbelief as Yvan Cournoyer hugged Henderson, who danced in the air, his arms and stick raised in celebration. At that moment, photographer Frank Lennon captured an image said by one observer to be "etched into the visual cortex of every Canadian." Lennon's famous photo, along with Hewitt's call, conferred mythic status on The Goal and a series whose gut-wrenching emotion and high-calibre action still eclipses any NHL championship or the international hockey triumph of other nations.

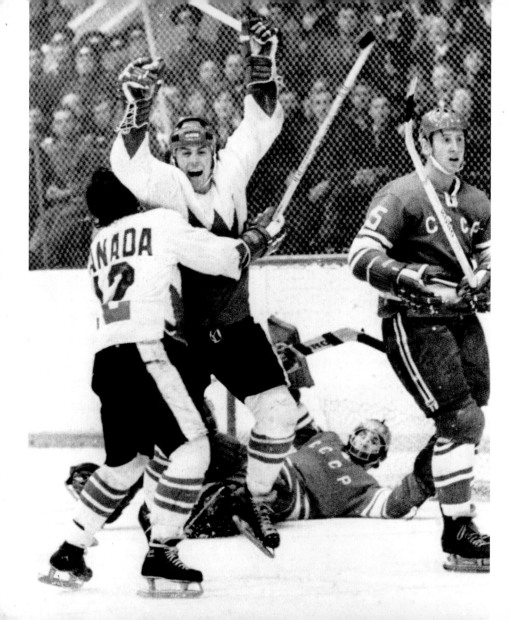

The series-clincher was no piece of art though, a whack-and-hack goal delivered from a scramble. But in the context of the times, as Cold War tensions raged and the game's two superpowers collided for the first time, the winning goal was more than just about hockey. For many, Canada was defending not only its national game, but also the very principles the country lived by. As writer William Houston noted, Henderson's winner "announced to the world that he had scored the goal for democracy." As melodramatic as that might sound today, the showdown against the Soviets became a symbolic war of superiority between rival political systems. "They were the big, bad Russians, and I hated their guts," Henderson said later. "It was our way of life against their way of life." Yet as deeply as his goal moved people, it is what the series and Canada's win did for hockey that make it the greatest goal ever. More than a cathartic celebration for the home side, ultimately, the Summit Series transformed hockey itself, triggering exhibition NHL tours by European teams, the importing of Europeans into the WHA and the use of the Soviets' playing style and training methods by coaches in both the minor and pro leagues. The slim margin of victory proved that the North American game had a lot to learn from European hockey. In time, these tournaments and merging techniques produced a new hybrid style of play that we call today the world game.

MIRACLE ON ICE

Mike Eruzione, USA, February 22, 1980

The sounds and images still crackle with exhilarating energy. The famous chilling call of Al Michaels: "Do you believe in miracles?" Captain Mike Eruzione's heart-stopping goal: a snapshot fired from outside the Soviet faceoff circle. And the defining photo: Team USA's jubilant embrace at the Olympic Center in Lake Placid. Few events in sport have influenced the game in one country as much as that stunning triumph in 1980. A generation of kids was inspired to play hockey. The man responsible was Herb Brooks, whose own failure as a player to make the US national team in 1960, pushed him to coach a bunch of college players to the pinnacle of glory 20 years later. Brooks' Olympic bid was perhaps the finest coaching performance in American sports. Against the Soviets, a team that made a mockery of the Olympics' amateur-only status, USA came back three times from one-goal deficits. Then, in the third period, Buzz Schneider fired a long shot at goalie Vladimir Myshkin, who made the save and slid the puck into the far corner. It came back to a trailing Eruzione, who, from 20 feet out, blew a shot past the arm of Myshkin. Sheer bedlam. The Americans had seized the moment. They hung on to win 4–3 and earn a final game berth. Two days later, after beating Finland, USA won Olympic gold.

THE GOLDEN GOAL

Sidney Crosby, Canada, February 28, 2010

Late in the gold-medal game between Canada and USA at the 2010 Winter Olympics, Sidney Crosby failed to cash in on a breakaway that would have put Canada up 3–1 and clinched the victory. The missed opportunity loomed large when Zach Parise tied the score with 24 seconds left to force sudden-death overtime. The setback only added to the frustration that Crosby had been experiencing in the tournament. The Canadian superstar had scored just twice in his team's previous six games and had gone pointless in the first 60 minutes of this one. But Crosby, who is famous for his sense of dramatics, found salvation just past the seven-minute mark of OT, when he chipped the puck along the boards to winger Jarome Iginla, then wheeled toward the net and screamed, "Iggy! Iggy!" Although he had defender Ryan Suter draped all over him, Iginla slipped a pass back to Crosby, who had a direct path toward goalie Ryan Miller. Crosby did not hesitate, whipping a low shot through Miller's pads. The goal was greeted by an eruption of sound that spread though the arena and out into the streets of Vancouver and across the entire country. After the game, Team Canada centre Joe Thornton spoke for millions when he said, about Crosby, "You're just happy he's on your team. You're happy he was born in Canada. Thank God."

GRETZKY TO LEMIEUX

Mario Lemieux, Canada, September 16, 1987

It isn't considered the best hockey series just because Canada won. It's the best series because the Soviets agreed that they had never witnessed anything like it. Each country had assembled its strongest rosters from deep talent pools, with many key players in their prime. The best-of-three final was tied after two dramatic 6–5 overtime wins. In the championship match, the Big Red Machine came out flying before Canada clawed its way back to a 5–4 lead over two periods. Then, at 12:21 of the third frame, the Russians evened it. What came next is remembered by many to be the greatest rush ever. It started with Dale Hawerchuk tying up Vyacheslav Bykov on a crucial faceoff in the Canadian end, then Bykov collided with Valeri Kamensky, losing the puck. Mario Lemieux was there and chipped it ahead past a pinching Igor Kravchuk. Lemieux leaped around him and fed a backhand pass to Wayne Gretzky, with Larry Murphy on the wing. Canada now had a three-on-one break into the Soviet zone. Gretzky faked out Igor Stelnov by using Murphy as a decoy and then slipped it back to a trailing Lemieux, who buried a high wrister behind Sergei Mylnikov's glove hand. It was grand theatre—high drama between archrivals in the international spotlight. Canada's last-minute heroics won it, but the real winner was the world game.

ORR SOARS

Bobby Orr, Boston Bruins, May 10, 1970

There was little doubt that the Boston Bruins were going to win the 1970 Stanley Cup. Boston had outclassed the St. Louis Blues in the final's first three tilts, winning 6–1, 6–2 and 4–1. But Game 4, played on a 93°F Sunday afternoon at the steamy Boston Garden, was a tighter affair, and the two teams left the ice after 60 minutes tied 3–3. In overtime, Boston quickly pressed the attack, hemming St. Louis in its own end. Bobby Orr gambled, pinching in and stopping a clearing attempt by Larry Keenan. Orr sent the puck to Derek Sanderson at the end boards, then broke for the net. Sanderson hit No. 4 with a return pass and the 22-year-old sensation flipped the puck past goalie Glenn Hall for the Cup winner. As Orr shot, Blues defenseman Noel Picard lifted Orr's leg, propelling him upward. The iconic image of Orr flying through the air, his arms raised in jubilation, perfectly captured by Ray Lussier of the *Boston Herald*, is now regarded by many to be the most famous hockey photograph in history. The goal capped a dream season for Orr, who won the Art Ross Trophy as the NHL leading scorer, the Hart Trophy as league MVP, the Norris Trophy as top defenseman and the Conn Smythe Trophy as playoff MVP for his role in leading the Bruins to their first Stanley Cup triumph in 29 years.

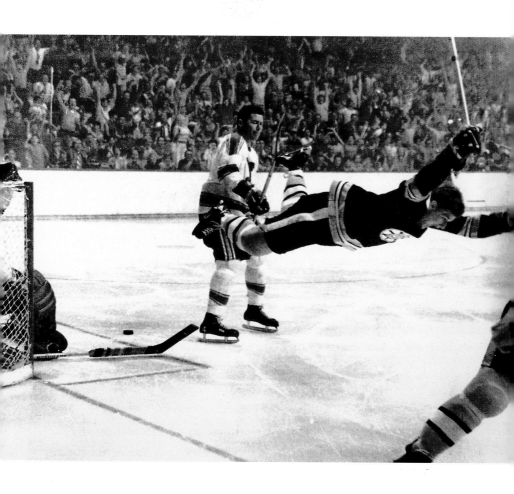

THE FASTEST 50

Wayne Gretzky, Edmonton Oilers, December 31, 1981

In the early stages of Wayne Gretzky's career, it appeared that the Oilers superstar could do just about anything he wanted on the ice. In 1980–81, Gretzky set his sights on breaking the record of 50 goals in 50 games, initially set by Maurice Richard in 1944–45 and equalled by Mike Bossy in 1979–80. Going into his 39th game of the season against Philadelphia, Gretzky had already netted 45, so the record was within reach, but nobody suspected it would fall that night, especially since the Flyers boasted one of NHL's best defenses. But apparently Gretzky had a hunch he would. As Paul Coffey told the *Edmonton Journal*, "Driving to the game that afternoon he said, 'I think I'm going to get five tonight.' I just looked at him and said, 'Alright, let's go.' It wasn't cocky. It wasn't arrogance, it was just a quiet confidence he had." That night, Gretzky ran wild. By his own admission, "I had eight or nine good chances. Their goalie [Pete Peeters] made some great saves." But in the end Peeters could do nothing to stop the historic tally. In the final minute, with the Flyers trailing 6–5, Peeters was on the bench for an extra attacker, when Glenn Anderson got control of the puck and skimmed it up the middle. Gretzky nabbed the disk, raced down ice, and shot it past a sprawling Bill Barber into the empty net for No. 50.

7

A NEW KING IS CROWNED

Wayne Gretzky, Los Angeles Kings, October 15, 1989

Six games into the 1989–90 season, Wayne Gretzky added another chapter to his illustrious legend, when he notched point number 1,851 to surpass Gordie Howe as the NHL's all-time scorer. Howe had reigned supreme atop the NHL scoring list since January 1960 and his record total, compiled over 26 seasons, had long seemed untouchable. But Gretzky destroyed that illusion, overtaking Howe early in his 11th season. Fittingly, Gretzky broke the record in Edmonton, the city where he had set so many of his previous scoring benchmarks. On this night, Gretzky began by picking up an assist on a Bernie Nicholls goal in the first period. Then, with his uncanny flair for the dramatic, he broke Howe's mark with only 53 seconds left in regulation. A point shot hit Dave Taylor's skate and deflected right to Gretzky's stick. He was alone on the doorstep and made no mistake, beating netminder Bill Ranford with a backhand that tied the game 4–4. Howe, who had been following the Kings around for days in anticipation of the milestone, came out to take part in a ceremony honouring the NHL's new point king. The superstitious would argue that it was fated to happen exactly the way it did. You see, Gretzky had scored his first NHL goal against Vancouver 10 years and a day earlier on October 14, 1979. The time of the goal was 18:51.

FIFTY-IN-FIFTY

Maurice Richard, Montreal Canadiens, March 18, 1945

The goal wasn't any more spectacular than hundreds of others scored by Maurice Richard during his storied 18-year career. It came on a simple pass from linemate Elmer Lach and was executed by Richard with pinpoint accuracy and velocity, two trademarks of the fiery play that made him a hockey legend. On this occasion, the puck eluded Boston goalie Harvey Bennett with less than three minutes left in Richard's sophomore campaign of 1944–45. Of course, what made this one famous was its number: 50—an unheard-of aggregate. And it came in a goal-a-game pace of 50 games. Although bettered several times since, Richard's triumph forever set the gold standard for snipers. Surprisingly, headlines of his feat were scant. More publicity came from Richard surpassing Joe Malone's goal record with his 45th marker weeks earlier and of Lach's new league mark of 54 assists, than of the Rocket's landmark 50-in-50. And although the magic 50-goal plateau was finally scaled, when voters picked the league MVP that year, the Hart Trophy went to scoring leader Lach, not Richard. It was the kind of snub that became all too familiar to Richard, a man who was to become both hero and villain, on and off the ice. An icon to an entire culture, he would not be defeated, intimidated nor dominated. It was the beginning of a legend.

ALONE AT THE TOP

Wayne Gretzky, Los Angeles Kings, March 23, 1994

At the start of the 1993–94 season, Wayne Gretzky needed only 37 goals to eclipse what many regarded as the NHL's greatest record—Gordie Howe's mark of 801 regular-season goals. In his prime, Gretzky would have been a cinch to exceed the standard by the All-Star break, but he had not scored 37 goals in either of his last two seasons and had only collected 16 the previous year, when he missed 39 games with a herniated disk. But slowly he closed in on the magic number, finally equalling his childhood idol's record with two goals against San Jose on March 20. In his next game, a home date with Vancouver, Gretzky could sense No. 802 coming. So could his wife, Janet, who told him before the game, "You know, this is going to be one of the highlights of your life. Make sure that you really sit back and enjoy it. Savour the moment." The moment came at 14:47 of the second period with the Kings on a power play. Luc Robitaille carried the puck over the Canucks blue line and dropped it back to Gretzky, who took a few strides and then zipped a cross-ice pass to a hard-charging Marty McSorley. As goalie Kirk McLean moved to his left, McSorley sent a return feed back to Gretzky, who was all alone at the left circle, and he calmly directed record-breaking goal No. 802 into the vacant cage.

HOWE SHOOTS DOWN THE ROCKET

Gordie Howe, Detroit Red Wings, November 10, 1963

There was a time when the debate about who was the NHL's best player involved only two players: Maurice Richard and Gordie Howe. Howe, who was seven years younger, was generally acknowledged as the best all-around performer, but Richard was considered the superior goal scorer, and so it was the Rocket's records that Howe was intent on tracking down. He became the NHL's career scoring leader when he passed Richard's 946 points on January 16, 1960. In 1962–63, the 35-year old Detroit icon won his sixth scoring title and also became the NHL's all-time leading goal scorer with 545, passing Richard again. The milestone moment came against Richard's former team, the Canadiens, while the Red Wings were killing off a five-minute penalty. Howe's teammate, Billy McNeill, took the puck inside the Detroit zone and headed up ice, with Howe trailing and yelling at him to keep going. After crossing Montreal's blue line, McNeill passed to Howe, who fired a dart through the narrow gap between goalie Charlie Hodge and the right post. The 15,027 fans in Detroit's Olympia Stadium gave their hero a 10-minute standing ovation. The goal left Howe, who had been feeling the pressure in his chase to pass the Rocket, more relieved than elated. "Now I can start enjoying life again," he said after Detroit's 3–0 win.

BILL'S THRILLER

Bill Barilko, Toronto Maple Leafs, April 21, 1951

Considering that the first four games of the 1951 Stanley Cup Final between Montreal and Toronto were decided in overtime, it surprised no one when Game 5 also went into sudden death. But what was unexpected was the scoring hero: "Bashing" Bill Barilko, a stay-at-home defenseman best known for his thundering bodychecks. Toronto, who led the series three games to one, tied the contest 2–2 on a goal by Tod Sloan with just 32 seconds left to play, setting the stage for Barilko's moment of glory. Early in overtime, Toronto's Howie Meeker retrieved the puck behind the Montreal net and poked it out in front to Harry Watson, who took a shot. As goalie Gerry McNeil stretched to stop it, the puck hit defenseman Butch Bouchard and caromed to the right side. Barilko suddenly came storming in from the blue line and took a swing at the puck, sending it into the top of the net over McNeil. As it hit the twine, Barilko continued on his headlong rush, for an instant entirely airborne. It was the last goal that Barilko would score. The 24-year-old vanished that summer on a fishing trip in northern Ontario. In an eerie twist, his body and the wreckage of his plane were not discovered until June 7, 1962, a month after the Leafs had defeated Chicago to end an 11-year Stanley Cup drought.

RECORD BLAST IN THE WINDY CITY

Bobby Hull, Chicago Blackhawks, March 12, 1966

The Rangers led the Blackhawks 2–1, but the fans at Chicago Stadium were not focused on the score. They were waiting for Bobby Hull to make history. The Chicago gunner was one goal shy of breaking the mystical NHL record of 50 goals in a season. Only three players in NHL history had ever scored 50 goals in a season, and all three—Maurice Richard, Bernie Geoffrion and Hull himself (1961–62, *see photo*)—had stopped at 50 as if that number represented some strange, impassable barrier. Gordie Howe once got to 49 goals with two games left to play but could not crack the mark. Early in the third, Hull took a pass, circled in his own zone and headed up ice. When he hit the Rangers blue line, Hull stopped, went into his big backswing and let fly. But instead of launching a screaming drive, he topped the puck and it came in at half speed, arriving at the crease just as Eric Nesterenko swooped in front of netminder Cesare Maniago and lifted his stick. The puck slid under Maniago's paddle and into the net. As the red light flashed, the Chicago crowd exploded. Hull stood alone on the ice, as the pipe organ roared and the cheers of 20,000 fans rained down along with hats, popcorn, programs and tickertape. The applause lasted seven noisy minutes. The 50-goal barrier had finally been breached.

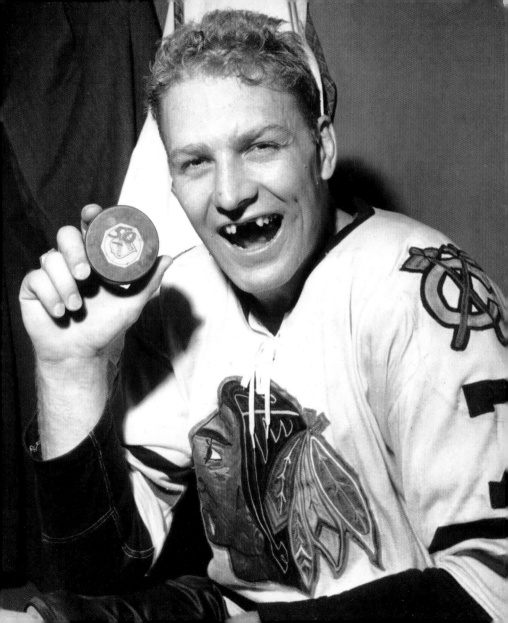

A DYNASTY IS BORN

Bob Nystrom, New York Islanders, May 24, 1980

There is a fine line between choker and champion. For a contending team, the difference is that ever-elusive missing piece to the Stanley Cup puzzle. It may be a new player, or just a key goal. For the dynasty New York Islanders, winners of four straight championships during the early 1980s, that player was centre Butch Goring; and the goal was Bob Nystrom's 5–4 overtime Cup winner in 1980. As coach Al Arbour said: "Until that moment, we were considered a team of losers and chokers. If Nystrom doesn't score, who knows what happens to our team?" For any coach, uttering the C-word is risky but the Isles had failed in four prior trips to the semifinals. Then, GM Bill Torrey acquired Goring in March 1980. The Islanders, with Arbour's airtight defense and big speedy offense, suddenly clicked after being poised for greatness for years. In the playoffs, they mowed down Los Angeles, Boston and Buffalo, before facing Philadelphia in a final series that ended with Nystrom's climactic winner in Game 6. Some felt the Flyers were robbed, with one Islander goal scored on a high stick and another on a blatant offside, but at 7:11 of overtime John Tonelli fed a perfect pass to a streaking Nystrom, who redirected it with a backhand shot past Pete Peeters. It started the longest Cup run by an American team in NHL history.

MARK MY WORDS

Mark Messier, New York Rangers, May 25, 1994

New York was down three games to two in the Eastern Conference Finals and facing elimination at the hands of the New Jersey Devils, when Rangers captain Mark Messier boldly guaranteed a win in Game 6. The New York media ate it up, but Messier's declaration looked like nothing but empty bravado with the hometown Devils holding a 2–0 lead late in the second period—until Messier stole the puck, burst into the Devils zone and dropped the puck to Alexei Kovalev, who ripped a shot past goalie Martin Brodeur. Then, early in the third, Messier flew by the New Jersey defense and whipped a backhander under Brodeur's left pad to tie the score. Nine minutes of pressure-cooker hockey passed before Messier struck again, bursting past Bernie Nicholls to stuff in a rebound at 12:12. However, New Jersey was not yet dead. After Rangers forward Glenn Anderson was penalized with 2:49 left to play, the Devils pulled Brodeur and began buzzing the Rangers net. The threat was snuffed out when Messier intercepted a pass and scaled the puck the length of the ice into the empty net to complete his natural hat trick. The captain had made good on his promise. When the Rangers beat New Jersey in Game 7, Messier's reputation as one of hockey's greatest leaders was indelibly etched in ice.

15

TRUE GRIT

Bobby Baun, Toronto Maple Leafs, April 23, 1964

The setting was the Detroit Olympia, Game 6 of the 1964 Stanley Cup Final. The Maple Leafs, trailing three games to two in the series, were locked in a 2–2 tie with Detroit with seven minutes remaining when defenseman Bobby Baun blocked a slapshot and crumpled to the ice. The Leafs rearguard was carried off on a stretcher and looked to be done for the series. In the dressing room, Baun stubbornly insisted on getting the damaged leg frozen and taped, and then returned to the action. Early in overtime, a puck deflected off George Armstrong's stick and came to Baun at the right point. He slapped at the rolling disk and sent a looping shot toward the Detroit net. The puck glanced off defenseman Bill Gadsby's stick and bounced into the net behind goalie Terry Sawchuk. Inspired by Baun's display of courage, the Leafs returned home for Game 7 and won 4–0, to cop a third straight Stanley Cup. Baun, "jazzed to the eyeballs with Novocaine," as *Globe and Mail* sportswriter Dick Beddoes put it, played the entire game. It was not until two days later that Baun consented to have his injured leg X-rayed. It was discovered that he had a hairline fracture of the fibula. The only NHL player to score an overtime playoff goal on a broken leg, Baun spent most of the summer wearing a cast.

MAGNIFIQUE

Mario Lemieux, Pittsburgh Penguins, May 17, 1991

The 1991 Stanley Cup Final pitted the Pittsburgh Penguins against the Cinderella-story Minnesota North Stars. In the first two playoff rounds, Minnesota had upset Chicago and St. Louis and then had annihilated the defending champion Edmonton Oilers in the Campbell Conference Finals. The visiting North Stars beat the Penguins 5–4 in Game 1 of the finals series, and appeared primed to go all the way when Mario Lemieux turned the tide in Game 2. With the Pens clinging to a 2–1 lead midway through the second period, Lemieux took a pass from Phil Bourque in his own zone and headed up ice as if propelled by rockets. As he reached the North Stars blue line, defensemen Shawn Chambers and Neil Wilkinson attempted to block his advance. Lemieux faked to his left and as soon as Chambers moved that way, the big centre put the puck through Chambers' legs, splitting the defense. As Chambers staggered backward, Lemieux went forehand to backhand, deking goaltender Jon Casey and stuffing the puck into the net as he crashed into the goal post. Said *Hockey Night in Canada* announcer Bob Cole: "Oh my goodness! What a move! What a goal! Lemieux! Oh baby!" The momentum of the series shifted on the play, and Pittsburgh cruised to a 4–1 win, eventually capturing the Cup in six games.

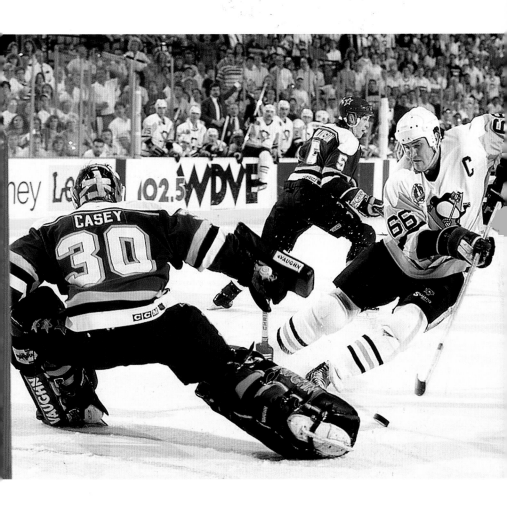

KILL SHOT

Guy Lafleur, Montreal Canadiens, May 10, 1979

Great goals are often remembered for their execution of play or grand achievement, and rarely for anything so mundane as a botched line change. But that is what most fans associate with Guy Lafleur's fabled tying goal against Boston during the 1979 playoffs. The Bruins had pushed the powerhouse Canadiens to a seventh game and were leading 4–3 with less than three minutes in regulation. A fourth consecutive Stanley Cup and a date in the final were on life-support. Then, the most famous too-many-men infraction in NHL history was called against Boston. Coach Don Cherry became the official goat, but Bruins winger Stan Jonathan was the real culprit. Then, Jacques Lemaire roared down the right wing and dropped the puck back to Lafleur, who was streaking up ice, his sweater billowing and blond hair rippling in his wake. In full stride he unleashed a laser beam between Gilles Gilbert's leg pad and the far post. Gilbert kicked hard to make the save, but missed and fell backwards, his body splayed out on the ice in surrender posture for what seemed to be, well, roughly forever. He knew. Everyone knew. The net bulged, the red light flashed and the crowd, hypnotized by the moment, suddenly erupted with an ear-splitting roar. "Did you ever stop a bullet? I never did. And I never will," Gilbert still says.

THE RIFLEMAN

Teemu Selanne, Winnipeg Jets, March 2, 1993

Few players have ever had a more dramatic impact on the NHL than Teemu Selanne did in his rookie season. The 22-year-old winger burst out of the gate like a prize greyhound, notching 30 goals in his first 38 games. By late February, he had scored 51 goals in just 63 games and was closing in on Mike Bossy's 1977–78 rookie record of 53 goals. On March 2 at Winnipeg Arena, Selanne shattered Bossy's mark with flair, scoring three times against the Quebec Nordiques. His third goal, the record-breaking 54th, came after Jets winger Tie Domi hoisted a long, floating pass that bounced crazily toward the Quebec goal. Nordique defenseman Adam Foote stumbled, allowing a streaking Selanne to zip past him towards the Quebec net. Goalie Stéphane Fiset opted to come out and attempt to swat the skittering puck away from the onrushing Finn, but Selanne was too quick and deftly chipped the disk over the diving netminder and into the empty cage. The young sniper celebrated by wheeling around and tossing one glove aloft. Then he reversed his stick so it resembled a rifle and pretended to shoot the glove out of the air. With the record securely in his pocket, Selanne continued to light the lamp at a blistering pace, finishing the season with 76 goals, setting a rookie record that many call unbreakable.

THE UNCONSCIOUS GOAL

Maurice Richard, Montreal Canadiens, April 8, 1952

If any single goal defines the heroic greatness of Maurice Richard, it may well be his "unconscious" series winner against Boston during the 1952 semifinals. The Bruins had forced Montreal to a seventh game and a 1–1 score late in the third period. Although it was reportedly a clean, hard-fought match, Richard was still reeling from the impact of Leo Labine's ruthless charge during second-period play. The hit knocked him out, but Richard refused a hospital visit for X-rays. He returned just as coach Dick Irvin called a line change with four minutes left. Still groggy and bleeding from fresh stitch work above the left eye, Richard tumbled over the boards with Toe Blake and Elmer Lach. Within moments, he began his epic rush from deep in Habs territory. Acting on pure reflex, he eluded Fleming Mackell at the blue line, slipped around Woody Dumart and knifed his way through Boston defenders Bill Quackenbush and Bob Armstrong. It was like checking a phantom, as a possessed Richard button-hooked Armstrong and burst full-bore across the goalmouth to drive the winner past Sugar Jim Henry. The execution of play under pain brought a thunderous ovation from rafter to rinkside that lasted four minutes. Later, Richard apologized for not passing the puck to his mates, saying: "My eyes were blurry."

ALEXANDER THE GREAT

Alexander Ovechkin, Washington Capitals, January 16, 2006

Alexander Ovechkin has scored a number of incredible goals in his young NHL career, but none more astounding than the one he notched against Phoenix on January 16, 2006. The play began as the Russian rookie carried the puck down the right side, before cutting toward the centre of the ice. As he moved the puck to his backhand he was jolted by Coyotes defenseman Paul Mara and knocked off his feet. But as Ovechkin was falling he somehow managed to corral the sliding puck with the hook of his blade on his backhand. Then, the most unbelievable part: while sliding on his back and facing away from the net he blindly slipped the puck it into the net past sprawling goalie Brian Boucher. Ovechkin's refusal to give up on the play and his ability to score when it seemed all but impossible, made the goal an instant classic for hockey highlights. Among the thousands of awestruck viewers was Bill Clement, studio host for NBC's NHL coverage. "We were in our studio last night when word was passed down: 'Wait until you see this highlight. It may be the best goal this year.' Our jaws dropped," said Clement. "Oh my god. It's one of the greatest goals of all time." Ovechkin's reaction was more modest. "I was lucky," the 20-year-old winger told ESPN. "I never did it before. We win the game so right now we feel pretty good."

A SETTLING OF SCORES

Jaroslav Holik, Czechoslovakia, April 20, 1972

The most dramatic upset in international hockey may be Czechoslovakia's triumph at the 39th IIHF World Championships in 1972. The mighty Soviets had stockpiled nine consecutive championships and had hammered out three straight Olympic gold medals. But a different story emerged during competition when the Czechs tied Russia 3–3 and both nations had won all their other games. Now, nothing was assured in the showdown match for the world title. Although the Soviets were superior at every position, the Czechs had an emotional edge. The host city was Prague, where bloody battles had erupted just four years earlier during the Russian invasion of 1968. With civil resistance futile, Czech nationals turned to hockey for revenge. Payback came in a highly charged 3–2 victory on home ice on a goal by Jaroslav Holik, who, ironically, just returned after a lengthy suspension for his anti-Soviet statements. Holik, the big brute of a centre whose aggressive style at both ends of the rink earned top points and penalties throughout his career, lumbered in on a partial two-on-one break and, rather than pass to his open man, fired from between the faceoff circles, beating netminder Vladislav Tretiak. Holik's goal brought the whole country together in celebration and today remains a defining moment in Czechoslovakian hockey history.

THE ROCKET'S RED GLARE

Maurice Richard, Montreal Canadiens, October 19, 1957

He played each game with blazing passion and boundless daring, yet even Maurice Richard was left stunned for a split-second at his achievement. It all happened so quickly, beginning with a penalty to Chicago defenseman Ian Cushenan, who was nailed for holding Richard on one of his lightning sorties into the Blackhawks zone. That brought out the Canadiens power play with Dickie Moore, Jean Béliveau and Richard up front. Moore started the play with a pass to Béliveau, who was lurking near the side of Chicago's net. Richard, signaling for the puck, stood about 15 feet out in front of goalie Glenn Hall. Béliveau played it to Richard. He one-timed it and the slapshot screamed past Hall only a few inches off the ice. The Chicago netminder could only flinch before the red light flashed. As if wired to the goal light itself, the sellout crowd of 14,405 fans lurched from their seats simultaneously in a standing ovation that engulfed the Montreal Forum for a full minute. Richard threw his stick in the air and embraced Béliveau and Moore. Then, the organist played "Il a Gagné ses Epaulettes" ("He's Earned His Stripes") and finally the announcement from Forum public address man Jacques Belanger: "Canadiens goal scored by Mr. Hockey himself, Maurice Richard." The NHL had its first 500-goal man.

SVERIGE 1995

VM I ISHOCKEY 3 70

G. HERSHORN · I. SJÖÖBLOM SC

HIGH NOON AT LILLEHAMMER

Peter Forsberg, Sweden, February 27, 1994

The goal was daring, inspired and flawlessly executed; the kind of virtuoso performance that defines the Olympic ideal of greatness. It came in a wild shootout after 60 minutes of regulation and 10 minutes of overtime in a 2–2 deadlock between Canada and Sweden. On the 13th shot, Peter Forsberg moved in on Corey Hirsch, rolled to his left, pulled the Canadian netminder with him, and then nimbly slipped the puck from his forehand to his backhand and with one glove on his stick tucked the puck under the arm of a sliding Hirsch and into the open net. When Paul Kariya then missed on his attempt, Sweden won gold in Lillehammer. Although the shootout was riveting entertainment, it was no way to determine the world's best team. Still, in a solo effort of just five seconds, Forsberg produced one of the most celebrated images in world hockey. For Hirsch, who played every minute of the tournament for Canada and faced twice the shot count of counterpart Tommy Salo in a 42-shot Swedish barrage, losing in the shootout was a bitter pill. Later, when Forsberg's goal was immortalized on a postage stamp, Hirsch refused to allow his likeness to be used, a decision he later regretted. So Sweden cast its national hero scoring on an unidentified goalie who wore a blue jersey instead of red, and No. 11 instead of Hirsch's No. 1.

ONE GOAL IN MIND

Jarome Iginla, Canada, February 24, 2002

The message delivered in Canada's dressing room before 2002's gold-medal game against USA was succinct: "Gentlemen, losing is not an option." Those exact words weren't used but the tone was set by Mario Lemieux, Steve Yzerman and others who came to the Olympics with one goal in mind: gold. Everyone in that room believed, but Canada's aspirations had been thwarted before, most recently at 1996's World Cup of Hockey by American goalie Mike Richter's singular performance and then during the 1998 Olympics by Czech goalie Dominik Hasek. In fact, it had been 50 years of near-misses, hot netminders and what-ifs since the Edmonton Mercurys claimed gold in 1952. It was as American foe Jeremy Roenick later admitted: Once the puck dropped, "you could tell they needed it. Fifty years of emotion was pent up in the way they played." But with just four minutes left, Canada led 3–2, no certainty against this poised US squad. Then, Joe Sakic and Yzerman combined on a pass to Jarome Iginla, who one-timed it at Richter, who misplayed the fluttering puck. It glanced off his glove into the air, fell in the crease, struck the inside post and trickled over the goal line. Another goal assured Canada the gold in the 5–2 victory. Everything was right for Canada, because anything less than total victory was unacceptable.

SWEDISH GOLD RUSH

Mats Sundin, Sweden, May 4, 1991

It's been recognized as the greatest goal of the World Championships. And, for Mats Sundin, few would argue any of his other goals, amateur or pro, have been bigger. Only 20 years old at the time, with one season of NHL experience, Sundin single-handedly brought Sweden gold in 1991 after a sensational coast-to-coast rush against the defending-champion Soviets. The score was tied 1–1 and 10 minutes remained in the final game. Sundin gathered the puck behind his own net and charged up the right side over his blue line, then deked around two Soviets like they were pylons, before crossing into his opponent's zone. The last skater back was legendary defenseman Vyacheslav Fetisov, one of international hockey's top rearguards. Sundin, the youngest player on the two teams, put a dazzling inside-out move on Fetisov that left the veteran defender flat-footed and more than a stride behind. In alone on Soviet goalie Andrei Trefilov, Sundin cocked and fired a wicked, low shot through the netminder's five-hole. Sweden hung on for a slim 2–1 victory and claimed championship gold on the streaking Swede's extraordinary play before a world audience at Turku, Finland. After being called a traitor by the Swedish media for joining the NHL 10 months earlier, Sundin returned home as the star of Tre Kronor and a national hero.

A DECLARATION OF WAR

Valeri Kharlamov, Soviet Union, September 2, 1972

The home of the storied Montreal Canadiens has witnessed a bounty of memorable games, but never before had there been a spectacle like Game 1 of the Summit Series at the Montreal Forum. Few there cared as much about the international game as they did about their beloved Habs, but in the Cold War of hockey against Russia, Canada ruled. Or so went the thinking. The game began as expected, with quick successive goals by Canada, but the Soviets tied it 2–2 after 20 minutes. Then, the myth of invincibility melted with the shocker authored by Valeri Kharlamov, an inventive forward of sublime skill who struck early in the second period with a goal that belied the Soviet stereotype of ice robot and gave his team a lead it would not relinquish. Kharlamov hit Canada's blue line, lowered his left shoulder as if to split the defense, then blew around Don Awrey's outside before cutting back inside, all with one hand on his stick cradling the puck. The Soviet sniper, in a stunning display of speed and agility, slid it back to his forehand, undressed Ken Dryden and flicked the shot through his five-hole. Suddenly, in the first temple of hockey, numb silence. Canada was losing. The on-ice swagger vanished, along with the comfort zone in the stands. The balance of power had shifted. War on ice had been declared.

SEVENTH HEAVEN

Mark Messier, New York Rangers, June 14, 1994

The champagne was chilling. The riot police were assembling. Anticipation crackled in the Manhattan air. The New York Rangers needed only one more win to claim the Stanley Cup and expunge the infamous curse that had plagued the franchise for 54 frustrating years. By game time, the crowd at Madison Square Garden was already chanting: "We Want the Cup!" Game 7 was a spine-tingler. New York took a two-goal lead, only to see Canucks captain Trevor Linden reply with a shorthanded breakaway goal early in the second period. With Vancouver pressing for the equalizer, the Rangers needed a break. They got it when Dave Babych was sent off for tripping at 12:36. Midway through the power play, after Canucks goalie Kirk McLean blocked shots by Adam Graves and Brian Noonan, the puck trickled to Messier, stationed at the left post. He swatted at it, and the puck deflected off a leg and rolled across the goal line. The crowd exploded, but there was still 40 minutes left. Linden, who was playing with cracked ribs and torn rib cartilage, scored again in the third to make it 3–2, but the Rangers staved off the Canucks' desperate attack. As the horn sounded and fireworks ignited, Messier danced a jig of joy. Behind him, a fan raised a sign that read, "Now I Can Die in Peace." The curse had been lifted.

THE HAT TRICK THAT CHANGED HOCKEY

Jean Béliveau, Montreal Canadiens, November 5, 1955

It is known as the "Montreal Canadiens rule," but it might as well be named after their long-time captain, Jean Béliveau. When Béliveau entered the NHL in 1953–54, league rules on minor infractions required a penalized team to play shorthanded for the entire two minutes, no matter how many goals were scored. The talent-laden Canadiens often put a game out of reach during a single power play by scoring multiple times. That situation soon changed after a Boston-Montreal game in November 1955 when referee Jerry Olinski whistled Cal Gardner and Hal Laycoe to the box with their Bruins up 2–0. Out trundled the Habs' top specialty unit, with Bert Olmstead and Béliveau. Outmanned by two and facing the league's most fearsome power play, Boston suffered the greatest PK meltdown ever as Béliveau erupted for three goals in a 44-second span against Terry Sawchuk, each goal coming from close-in with first assists by Olmstead. In just over a minute from Laycoe's penalty start, the Canadiens erased their 2–0 deficit and surged ahead 3–2. The Montreal Forum crowd cheered wildly. The Bruins became incensed and later GM Lynn Patrick appealed to league governors for a rule change that enabled a penalized player to return to the ice after an opponent scored. Today, it's still enforced as Rule 16.2.

THE "NO GOAL"

Brett Hull, Dallas Stars, June 19–20, 1999

Brett Hull's so-called "No Goal" against Buffalo in 1999 may be the most controversial goal in Stanley Cup history. The sweet irony is who *but* Hull should be the lightning rod on the long disputed goal? During his career, his mouth repeatedly got him in trouble with coaches and the league. Then, there was Hull's pivotal "high-stick" equalizer at 1996's World Cup of Hockey. Now, the Stars sniper was again in the crosshairs, this time for his Cup winner with his left skate planted squarely in Dominik Hasek's crease. All season, officials had disallowed such goals. And under existing rules, a goal was illegal if the offensive player entered the crease before the puck did. But the real debate hinged on whether Hull had control of the puck when he scored. The play started with Hull's tip-in attempt in the third OT period of Game 6. Hasek stopped it, but the rebound went back to Hull, who fired away again. Hasek, now down on the ice, made that stop. The puck squirted back into Hull's skates. He deftly kicked it onto his stick and shot it into the net. The red light went on, Hull's teammates mobbed him and the Cup was celebrated under great controversy. Hull, playing on torn ligaments, never received his due. Within days, the league tweaked the crease rule, allowing attacking players to score in the crease.

MISSION IMPOSSIBLE

Pete Langelle, Toronto Maple Leafs, April 18, 1942

We can add Pete Langelle to the list of improbable Stanley Cup heroes. Although the centre scored only 22 regular-season goals in his NHL career, he netted the goal that completed the most incredible comeback in finals history, as the Leafs rallied from a three-game deficit to defeat Detroit in 1942. Much of the credit for the turnaround goes to Toronto coach Hap Day, who shook up his roster for Game 4, benching several regulars, including scoring star Gordie Drillon. His replacement, rookie Don Metz, notched four goals and three assists in the next three games to help spark the Leafs to 4–3, 9–3 and 3–0 victories. In Game 7, a record Maple Leaf Gardens' crowd of 17,000 watched Detroit carry a 1–0 lead into the third when Sweeney Schriner finally solved goalkeeper Johnny Mowers with 12:14 left. Two minutes later, Langelle's line, with Bob Davidson on left wing and Johnny McCreedy on the right side, stormed into the Red Wings zone. McCreedy blasted a shot on Mowers, who moved far out to deflect the drive, but the puck rebounded back into play, and Mowers was stranded. Langelle pounced on the disk and smacked it into the yawning cage to put the Leafs up 2–1. Schriner added a late insurance goal and Toronto had done the impossible— come all the way back to win the series.

A CLASSY THIEF

Frank Boucher, New York Rangers, April 14, 1928

New York Rangers classy centre Frank Boucher had been dubbed "Raffles" by sportswriter Andy Lytle after a famous fictional safecracker as a tribute to his puck-stealing ability, and in the spring of 1928 Boucher stole the Cup from the Montreal Maroons. The Rangers had no business winning that year. Not only did they have to play the entire series at Montreal because the circus had invaded Madison Square Garden, they also lost star goalie Lorne Chabot to an injury in Game 2, and had to finish the game with 44-year-old coach Lester Patrick between the pipes. New York won that famous game on an overtime goal by Boucher to even the best-of-five series. The Maroons prevailed in Game 3, but the Blueshirts rebounded to take the next contest 1–0 on another goal by Boucher. In Game 5, the Maroons poured it on, raking substitute goalie Joe Miller with shots, but it was Boucher who opened the scoring with one of only three Ranger shots in the first period. The Maroons tied it in the second, but Boucher restored New York's lead in the third, connecting on a breakaway as his team was killing off a penalty. It was a dagger to the heart. In all, Boucher scored four of the Rangers' five goals in the series and the game-winners in each of their three victories.

32

THE ASSASSIN'S TOUCH

Wayne Gretzky, Los Angeles Kings, May 29, 1993

In the first five games of the 1993 Western Conference Finals, the "Great One" was anything but. *Toronto Star* columnist Bob McKenzie wrote that he was "skating like he had a piano on his back." But the tune changed in Games 6 and 7 as Wayne Gretzky began hitting all the right notes. No. 99 torpedoed Toronto in Game 6, netting the winner in overtime. Then, in the deciding contest at Maple Leaf Gardens, he scored the night's first goal while Los Angeles was shorthanded, set up the second one, then scored again in the second after the Buds had fought back to tie the game. In the third, with the Kings clinging to a 4–3 lead, Gretzky stole the puck and moved into Toronto's end. As he circled behind the net, he saw that no teammate had joined him on the rush. Making something out of nothing, he backhanded the puck at Leafs defenseman Dave Ellett, who was guarding the front of the goal. The puck hit Ellett's skate and deflected past a shocked Felix Potvin, giving the "Great One" a hat trick. It was a huge goal for the Kings, because Toronto refused to die, jamming in another goal with a minute left to make it 5–4. As the seconds ticked down, the Leafs pulled Potvin and swarmed the Kings net in a frantic bid to score the equalizer, but time ran out and the boys from California celebrated.

THE LONG DRIVE

Eddie Shore, Boston Bruins, January 3, 1929

On January 2, 1929, Eddie Shore got caught in Boston traffic and missed the team train as the Bruins left for a game in Montreal against the Maroons. Unable to fly because of a sleet storm, he had a friend lend him a car and a driver. At 11:30 PM, Shore and the chauffeur headed north on a 350-mile trip over icy, snow-blocked New England mountains. It was sleeting and there were no paved superhighways, no road patrols and no sanders. Unhappy with the chauffeur's cautious pace, Shore took the wheel and drove to a service station, where he had tire chains put on. By then the storm had thickened into a blizzard and within minutes the lone wiper blade froze solid to the glass. "I couldn't see out the window," said Shore, "so I removed the top half of the windshield." At 5:30 PM the next day, he finally made it to the Bruins' hotel, eyes bloodshot, face frostbitten and windburned, his fingers set like claws after gripping the steering wheel so long. The exhausted rearguard napped for 30 minutes before heading to the Montreal Forum. Incredibly, aside from sitting out two minor penalties, Shore played the entire 60 minutes without relief, bashing Maroons players with abandon and scored the game's only goal, completing a rink-length dash by firing a wrist shot into the net at 8:20 of the second period.

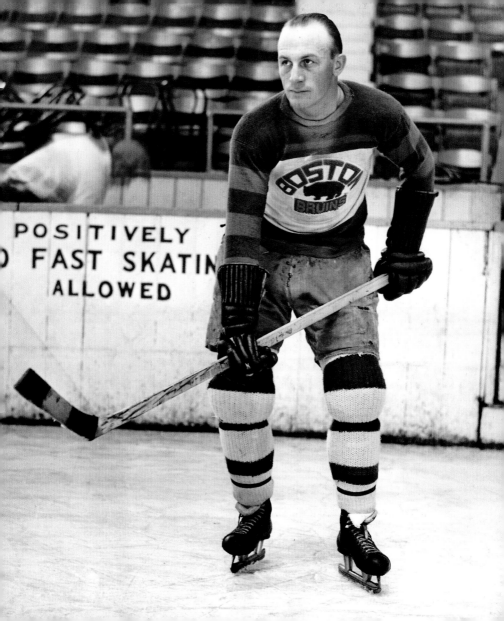
POSITIVELY
O FAST SKATIN
ALLOWED

WE HAVE LIFT-OFF

Pavel Bure, Vancouver Canucks, April 30, 1994

Pavel Bure dazzled Vancouver Canucks fans from the very beginning. In his NHL debut on November 5, 1991, Bure showcased his talent and speed with several electrifying end-to-end rushes that left a trail of Winnipeg Jets in his wake. As Trevor Linden noted about his explosive teammate, "Pavel was the type of player who could literally bring people out of their seats. He just made things happen when you didn't think anything could happen." It was during the seventh-seeded Canucks run to the 1994 Stanley Cup Final that Bure scored one of the most significant goals in club history. Early in the second overtime period of Game 7 of Vancouver's opening-round series against Calgary, he took a long pass from defenseman Jeff Brown, pulled away from Zarley Zalapski's hook and burst in alone on goalie Mike Vernon. The "Russian Rocket" deked right and went left, tucking the puck into the corner of the net to complete a hat trick and propel the Canucks on to the next round. Bure's sudden-death goal capped a remarkable comeback in which his club rallied from a three-games-to-one deficit with three consecutive overtime wins. Although Vancouver eventually fell one goal short of the Cup, losing 3–2 to the Rangers in Game 7 of the final, Bure's clutch goal remains a franchise high point.

SITTLER SEALS THE DEAL

Darryl Sittler, Canada, September 15, 1976

The finest collection of skill players ever assembled from the top six hockey nations gathered for the 1976 Canada Cup, and who among the brain trust behind the benches devised the winning strategy but lunch-pail assistant coach Don Cherry. The best-of-three final pitted Canada against reigning world champion Czechoslovakia. The Czechs were blanked in the first game 6–0, before rallying in the next match with a 4–4 tie in regulation. In the overtime intermission, Cherry suggested that any player on a breakaway against goalie Vladimir Dzurilla should fake a slapper and "if you see him come out of his net, draw it back in and go wide and deep." Darryl Sittler, who had three goals in six games, noted Grapes' observation and used it on a beautiful solo effort for the series winner. A little after 11 minutes of overtime, Marcel Dionne hit Sittler streaking in across the blue line. He had defenseman Jiri Bubla beaten on the left side but did not have enough room to cut back across the net, so Sittler tried Cherry's gambit. He faked a slapshot on Dzurilla, and as predicted, the Czech netminder came out, committing himself beyond the crease. Sittler took two more strides to the outside and wristed the puck into the open net to give Canada a 5–4 victory in the first true international best-on-best event.

BABANDO'S BLING

Pete Babando, Detroit Red Wings, April 23, 1950

How big was Pete Babando's playoff goal in 1950? Imagine if Marc-André Fleury hadn't made that diving stop on Nicklas Lidström in the final frantic seconds of Game 7 at the 2009 Stanley Cup Final. Detroit would have tied it 2–2 and taken Pittsburgh into sudden-death overtime to decide the championship. Imagine that. Under this scenario, had Lidström scored, history would be on the Red Wings' side in the extra session. The Wings are the only team ever to play a seventh game overtime in the Cup final. They've been there twice and each time they've prevailed, with a victory in 1954 on Tony Leswick's fluke goal against Montreal and, four years earlier, in 1950 with the Babando winner. In that Game 7, Detroit tied New York 3–3 late in the third period, and although the Wings carried the attack in the first overtime, neither side scored. Then, midway through the second session, Detroit's George Gee took a crucial draw against Buddy O'Connor to the left of Ranger goalie Chuck Rayner. Gee had instructed Babando to move behind him once the puck was dropped. Gee beat O'Connor to the draw and flicked it back to Babando, who shot it through a maze of players. Rayner kicked out his left pad, but the puck sailed into the far side of the net. It was the NHL's first sudden-death tally in a Game 7 for the Stanley Cup.

THE TURNING POINT

Mark Messier, Edmonton Oilers, May 15, 1984

In the 1984 Stanley Cup Final, the Edmonton Oilers faced the daunting challenge of defeating the mighty New York Islanders, winners of four straight Cups and a record 19 consecutive playoff series. Sparked by Grant Fuhr's stellar goaltending, the youthful Oilers squeezed out a 1–0 road win in Game 1, only to be rudely spanked 6–1 in Game 2 as the Islanders reasserted their dominance. The Oilers, who badly needed to win at home in Game 3 to restore their confidence, found themselves trailing 2–1 in the second period and struggling to mount an offense against the Islanders' suffocating checking. The turning point of the series came at the 8:38 mark, when Mark Messier brought the Northlands Coliseum crowd to its feet by deking defenseman Tomas Jonsson out of his underwear and then burning goalie Billy Smith with a wicked wrist shot to the short side. Messier's stunning effort energized his team, which then proceeded to pump in five unanswered goals in a span of 10 minutes and 19 seconds to win the crucial contest 7–2. The surging Oilers then went on to clobber the Islanders 7–2 and 5–2 to capture the series and the Cup. Afterwards, in the champagne-soaked Oilers' dressing room, defenseman Paul Coffey told reporters, "Messier's goal in Game 3 turned us into the team we had to be."

LEAP OF FAITH

Bobby Clarke, Philadelphia Flyers, May 9, 1974

Despite having lost Gerry Cheevers, Derek Sanderson and Johnny McKenzie to the WHA, the Boston Bruins were favoured to defeat the Philadelphia Flyers in the finals and win the 1974 Stanley Cup. The Bruins boasted the NHL's top four scorers during the regular season and had owned Philadelphia in head-to-head play. The Flyers had only beaten Boston once in franchise history and had never won in Boston. The Bruins won the series opener 3–2 on a late goal by Bobby Orr, and held a 2–0 lead after the first period of Game 2, when the Flyers rallied on goals by Bobby Clarke in the second and André "Moose" Dupont with just 52 seconds left in the third. The clubs then battled through 12 minutes of overtime until Clarke, described by *Sports Illustrated*'s Mark Mulvoy as "a gap-toothed diabetic rink rat with the guts of 10 dozen burglars," took a pass and backhanded the puck at the Bruins net. Gilles Gilbert made the save, but the Flyers captain retrieved the rebound and buried the game-winner to steal away Boston's home-ice advantage. His goal inspired the Flyers to go on to take the Cup in six games. "For the past few years," said Philadelphia goaltender Bernie Parent, "Boston was dominating the Flyers, but it all turned around with that one win in the playoffs."

Denis Savard, Chicago Blackhawks, February 24, 1988

Broadcaster Danny Gallivan coined the term "Savardian spin-a-rama" to describe a trademark move made by Montreal defenseman Serge Savard in which he'd do a full 360-degree turn with the puck to protect it from checkers. But today the term is most closely associated with centre Denis Savard, who often used the manoeuvre while in full flight to escape defenders and confuse goalkeepers. During his prime with Chicago, Savard was one of hockey's most masterful puckhandlers, and in this particular 1988 game he offered a stunning display of his wizardry while killing a penalty against the defending champion Edmonton Oilers. Savard was always pumped to play against Edmonton because Oilers coach Glen Sather had cut Savard from Team Canada in 1984, and in this game he got some revenge. After intercepting a pass at his own blue line, Savard whirled and danced around no less than four Oilers, evading Glenn Anderson (twice), then Esa Tikkanen and Kevin Lowe—before flipping the puck past goalie Grant Fuhr just as Tikkanen hauled him down from behind. Savard's shorthanded tally broke a 3–3 tie and sparked the Blackhawks to a 5–4 win. In 2009, TSN rated it as the greatest goal of all time in one of its Top 10 roundups. Although we won't go that far, the goal's wow factor certainly earns it a top billing.

ORR'S IMMACULATE PASS

Johnny Bucyk, Boston Bruins, March 22, 1973

The goal was scored by Johnny Bucyk, but the Bruins winger didn't have much to do other than swat the puck into an open net. No, what made this goal great wasn't the finish, but rather the amazing set-up supplied by Bobby Orr. The play began with Orr lugging the puck out of his own end and through centre ice with Minnesota North Stars centre Charlie Burns hounding him every step of the way. Orr pulled free of Burns at Minnesota's blue line and angled toward the centre of the ice where the defense corps of Fred Barrett and Barry Gibbs converged on him, blocking his route to the net. As they moved forward, Bucyk knifed in behind them on the left wing, ready to receive a pass from Orr, but before he could deliver the feed, Barrett cross-checked the Boston star, knocking him on his keister. Scoring chance denied, right? Well, not exactly. As Orr slid on his back toward the left faceoff circle, he nudged the puck to his stick blade with his elbow, and then with Burns still hacking at him, twisted around on the ice and sent a hard no-look pass *behind his back* toward Bucyk, who was cutting across the crease—and to his credit, watching Orr over his shoulder. The puck *hit the tape* on Bucyk's stick and the veteran quickly stuffed the disk past North Stars netminder Gilles Gilbert.

THE SAVIOUR

John Tonelli, New York Islanders, April 13, 1982

Although overshadowed by teammates Bryan Trottier and Mike Bossy, winger John Tonelli was an integral part of the Islanders' dynasty teams of the 1980s. Tonelli's two most memorable playoff goals were scored in the same game in 1982, as the Isles attempted to win a third straight Stanley Cup. New York had finished the 1981–82 season with 118 points, 43 more than its first-round playoff opponents, the Pittsburgh Penguins, and looked like a lock to win, especially after crushing the Penguins by scores of 8–1 and 7–2 in the first two games. But Pittsburgh battled back to even the series. In Game 5, the Pens led 3–1 with only five minutes left in the third, when Tonelli assisted on a Mike McEwen goal to make it 3–2. Then, with only 90 seconds remaining, a dump-in by Gord Lane hopped over Randy Carlyle's stick directly to Tonelli, who buried the puck behind goalie Michel Dion to force overtime. Six minutes into sudden death, McEwen blocked a shot and sent a breakaway pass to Tonelli. En route to the net, the bearded winger was dragged down by Paul Baxter and slid toward the corner. Tonelli scrambled to his feet and centred the puck to Bob Nystrom, who took a shot from close in. It was blocked by Dion, but Tonelli jammed home the rebound to win the series. Having survived that scare, New York went on to win the Cup.

LEMIEUX COMES BACK

Mario Lemieux, Pittsburgh Penguins, March 2, 1993

It was the goal that sparked the greatest comeback by an individual in hockey history. Arguably, it's the finest comeback in sports, one that transcends the game itself and certainly defies all normal athletic parameters. During his 1992–93 bid to eclipse Wayne Gretzky's record 215-point total, Mario Lemieux was diagnosed with Hodgkin's disease— cancer of the lymph nodes. Following months of radiation, Lemieux returned March 2 against Philadelphia. Although his energy level was sapped by the cumulative effects of the treatments, it wasn't evident as Lemieux played 20 minutes and scored a goal and an assist—all this coming after his final blast of radiation that morning. The goal came from the Flyers faceoff circle, when Lemieux ripped a sharp-angle wrist shot past Dominic Roussel. During the next 20 games he amassed 56 points to win the scoring crown with 160 points, 12 more than Pat LaFontaine. No scoring champion has ever played a lower percentage of games, just 60 of 84 matches, or 71 percent. Spread over 82 games, Lemieux's totals would have smashed Gretzky's illustrious goal and point records. And the Penguins built the longest win streak in NHL history: 17 games. Lemieux had fashioned one of the NHL's greatest scoring seasons—all done with a wonky back and cancer in remission.

MARATHON MAN

Modere "Mud" Bruneteau, Detroit Red Wings, March 24–25, 1936

"Gee whiz, that's swell," said wide-eyed Detroit rookie Mud Bruneteau as he turned the puck over and over in his hand. The prized disk had just been given to him by Montreal Maroons goalie Lorne Chabot on the afternoon following a record-setting marathon in the first game of the 1936 playoffs. After the heart-wrenching 1–0 loss, Chabot kept the puck as a souvenir, but figured it should go to Bruneteau, the night's hero who mercifully ended the match on the 158th shot at 16:30 of the *sixth* overtime period. The historic marker came at 176:30 on a broken play when Red Wings veteran Hec Kilrea misplayed the puck in the Maroons zone. The little used Bruneteau smartly gathered it up, repositioned himself and tucked the rolling puck into the net. After stopping 67 shots, the shell-shocked Chabot had no chance on the one that beat him. The Montreal Forum crowd of 9,000, themselves near the point of collapse, showed little objection, almost happy that it was finally over despite their team's loss. Even the goal judge was surprised. By the time the red light flashed, Chabot had left his crease for the dressing room. It was 2:25 AM and the NHL's longest match, almost three complete games, was over. Goalie Normie Smith made 90 saves, but the real star was Mud.

GOAL SHARK

Alexander Ovechkin, Washington Capitals, February 18, 2009

One thing is for certain: Alexander Ovechkin lives to score. "He's like the shark in *Jaws*, circling in the water, waiting for blood," noted John Davidson, president of the St. Louis Blues. "They should play that music from the movie—*da-duh, da-duh, da-duh*—when he's out on a shift. He doesn't just go after loose pucks, he hunts them down." In a 2009 game against Montreal, Ovechkin invented another novel way to score that left the crowd gasping in wonder. With his team down 1–0, he gobbled up an errant pass, then backhanded the puck to himself off the left boards—throwing in a 360-degree spin move to bamboozle defenseman Roman Hamrlik—and broke for the net. Kyle Chipchura hauled Ovechkin down as he tried to go around him with one hand on his stick, but the Russian still had enough body control to keep possession of the puck and flip it past goalie Carey Price while sliding on his backside. "I covered the bottom of the net the way I was supposed to, but somehow he managed to lift the puck when he was on his butt," said Price. So which one was better—this goal or the one Ovechkin scored in Phoenix in 2006? "I've seen that one about 1,000 times on TV," said Washington coach Bruce Boudreau, "but [tonight's goal] was as amazing a goal as I've ever seen."

LITTLE BIG MAN

Ken Doraty, Toronto Maple Leafs, April 4, 1933

Standing five foot seven and weighing only 135 pounds, Ken Doraty was one of the smallest players to lace up skates in the NHL. But the nimble little winger scored one of the biggest goals in playoff annals. The 26-year-old rookie brought the curtain down on one of the most gruelling playoff series in history, a war of attrition waged by the Boston Bruins and Toronto Maple Leafs in the 1933 semifinals. The first three games of the best-of-five affair were all decided in overtime, with Boston winning twice by 2–1 scores and the Leafs taking the other contest 1–0. In Game 4, the Leafs won 5–3, setting the stage for an epic Game 5 in Toronto. The marathon began at 8:30 PM and did not end until 1:48 the next morning. The players were so weary after the fifth overtime period that some wanted to settle the game by a coin flip. But NHL president Frank Calder ordered them to play on. The end finally came after 164 minutes and 46 seconds of shutout hockey, when a pass by Bruins immortal Eddie Shore was intercepted by Andy Blair. The Leaf centre shovelled the puck to Doraty, who beat goalie Tiny Thompson with a wrist shot, sending the crowd into a frenzy. As his teammates rushed to congratulate him, Doraty dove into the net to retrieve the puck, a souvenir of the longest game ever played at Maple Leaf Gardens.

"MATTEAU! MATTEAU! MATTEAU!"

Stéphane Matteau, New York Rangers, May 27, 1994

The New York Rangers had a talent-laden team in 1993–94, featuring such names as Mark Messier, Brian Leetch, Alexei Kovalev, Steve Larmer and Adam Graves. One player not on that All-Star list was Stéphane Matteau: the burly forward was a tireless worker, but he had hands of stone. In three seasons with the Blueshirts, Matteau counted a paltry 11 goals. Yet without his clutch contributions in the Eastern Conference Finals, the Rangers would not have won the Cup in 1994. Matteau posted the game-winning goal against New Jersey in double overtime of Game 3, and was the man of the moment in Game 7's double overtime. Coach Mike Keenan's skaters pressed the attack in overtime, but the Devils held fast and the game went into a second extra session. The decisive play happened suddenly. Matteau swooped in and beat Scott Niedermeyer to a loose puck on the left boards, carried it behind the Devils' cage and emerged on the other side, where his pass-out attempt hit goalie Martin Brodeur and deflected into the net. The goal was immortalized by New York announcer Howie Rose's memorable call. "Matteau! Matteau! Matteau! Stéphane Matteau! The New York Rangers are headed to the Stanley Cup Final where they have one more hill to climb baby, and that's Mount Vancouver!"

CAPTAIN COURAGEOUS

Paul Kariya, Anaheim Mighty Ducks, June 7, 2003

Somebody call a doctor! Paul Kariya definitely needed medical attention after he was flattened by a vicious, blindside hit early in the second period of Game 6 of the 2003 Cup final. A hush fell over the Arrowhead Pond arena as Anaheim's $10-million man lay motionless on his back for a minute before being helped to the dressing room. Kariya had been levelled by Scott Stevens, the New Jersey bell ringer who had knocked out Philadelphia's Eric Lindros with a bone-crushing check during a 2000 playoff game. Lindros sat out an entire season with a concussion, but Kariya made a much quicker return, rejoining the action five minutes later. Then he answered the critics who had been openly questioning his heart and lack of production. After being held without a goal in the first five games of the series, the Ducks captain finally broke his slump, taking a pass from Petr Sykora and rifling a slapshot from above the left circle that streaked by Martin Brodeur and inside the far post. It gave his team a three-goal lead and a major emotional boost. Inspired by Kariya's display of intestinal fortitude, Anaheim went on to win 5–2. Even Brodeur had to applaud. "It definitely showed a lot of grit for him to come back from a hit like that," said the Devils goalie after the game. "There are not too many guys who can do that."

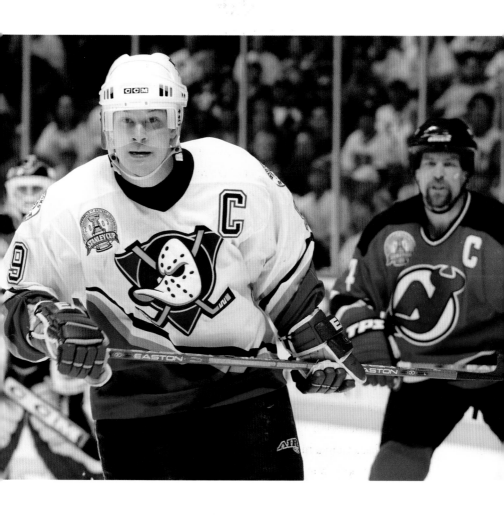

WORKING OVERTIME

Mel Hill, Boston Bruins, April 2, 1939

The 1939 semifinal between the Boston Bruins and New York Rangers had it all—fast-paced hockey, clutch goaltending, high drama and a surprising scoring hero. The entire round lasted more than nine hours and 13 minutes, making it the longest series in terms of total playing time in NHL annals. The Bruins won the first three tilts, the first two on sudden-death goals by 140-pound rookie winger Mel Hill, but the Rangers refused to quit, rebounding to take the next three and set up a winner-take-all contest at Boston Garden. Once again the teams went to overtime, deadlocked 1–1, and just like in Game 1, they battled through two scoreless periods before Hill again stole the spotlight. "It was around eight minutes of the third overtime," Hill recalled in an interview. "Bill Cowley fed me a pass from behind the net and I was right on top of Rangers goalie Bert Gardiner. I held the puck for a second then flipped it up into the net on the short side. The fans went wild and it was a tremendous thrill to win a series for my team." Hill's feat of scoring three overtime goals in one playoff series made him an overnight legend and earned him the nickname "Sudden Death." It was also sweet vindication for Hill, who had originally been cut by Rangers GM Lester Patrick because he felt the forward was "too frail for big-time hockey."

STICKING IT TO THE KINGS

Eric Desjardins, Montreal Canadiens, June 3, 1993

Ranking high on the roster of unlikely playoff stars is defenseman Eric Desjardins. Although Desjardins scored only 136 goals in 1,143 career games, he owns the distinction of netting the only hat trick by a defenseman in a Stanley Cup Final. The unexpected offensive salvo occurred in Game 2 of the Montreal–Los Angeles series in 1993; and it proved to be huge. With Montreal trailing 2–1 late in the third period, and down by a game in the series, coach Jacques Demers asked for a measurement of the stick of Kings defenseman Marty McSorley. The gamble paid off. The curve of his stick was deemed illegal and McSorley was given a two-minute minor. Since it was late in the game and Montreal was facing the prospect of going to L.A. down two games to zero, Demers opted to pull goalie Patrick Roy for a six-on-four advantage. In dramatic fashion, Desjardins scored on a screen shot from the point to tie the game and force overtime. Then, just 51 seconds into the overtime, Desjardins struck again, scoring the goal that turned the series. He swooped in to take a pass from Ed Ronan and beat Kelly Hrudey between the pads to give Montreal the victory and the momentum heading into Games 3 and 4 at the Great Western Forum. Riding that surge, the Habs swept the next three games to claim the Cup.

GRETZKY'S DAGGER

Wayne Gretzky, Edmonton Oilers, April 21, 1988

Fresh off winning the President's Trophy as the top team during the regular season, the Calgary Flames were favoured over the Edmonton Oilers for the first time in a playoff series. But Edmonton opened the division semifinals with a 3–1 win at Calgary's Olympic Saddledome. In Game 2, Calgary grabbed a 4–2 lead, only to see Edmonton rally and send the game to overtime. During intermission, Oilers coach Glen Sather told his team, "Go out and play to win. Don't lay back worrying about stopping them from scoring." The Oilers did just that, pressing the attack until Mark Messier picked up a penalty. The resulting power play gave the Flames a golden opportunity to even the series, but Wayne Gretzky turned the tables, corralling a loose puck and scooting down the left boards into the Flames zone. Cut off by an oncoming defenseman and with no one to pass to, Gretzky ripped a howitzer over goalie Mike Vernon's left shoulder into the top of the net. "You couldn't put that puck in there with a peashooter, but he put it in," marvelled Flames coach Terry Crisp. After the goal, Sather shook his fist at the silenced crowd and Gretzky shouted at the Saddledome ice attendants, telling them to take the ice out for the summer because the Flames would not need it anymore. And they wouldn't. The Oilers swept.

KEON COMES THROUGH

Dave Keon, Toronto Maple Leafs, April 9, 1964

The Toronto Maple Leafs and Montreal Canadiens have played many thrilling games in their storied rivalry, but Game 7 of the 1964 semi-finals was one of the best, a blistering exhibition of end-to-end rushes. Wrote *Globe and Mail* sports columnist Dick Beddoes: "You could have grated carrots on everybody's goose flesh and there were 14,541 noisy Montreal partisans perched on the wild edge of 14,541 cardiac conditions." Surprisingly, it was the visitors who dominated in the opening period, drawing first blood on a Dave Keon wrister from the slot. A few minutes later, as the Leafs were killing a penalty, Keon scored again, taking a pass from George Armstrong, outracing Jean-Guy Talbot and slapping a low drive past goalie Charlie Hodge. *Les Glorieux* regrouped in the intermission and came out flying, but could not solve 39-year-old goalkeeper Johnny Bower. In the third stanza they sent 18 shots his way but got just one over the line. Still, the contest remained in doubt until the waning seconds when Keon sealed the deal with his third of the night, an empty-netter. In a sombre Montreal dressing room after the game, coach Toe Blake confirmed the obvious, saying that Keon had killed them with his shorthanded breakaway tally. "That goal was the winner, and that was the break they needed."

COMEBACK ON MANCHESTER BOULEVARD

Daryl Evans, Los Angeles Kings, April 10, 1982

First their own fans booed them. And soon their opponents started laughing. Even their owner got up and left. But then a funny thing happened to the Los Angeles Kings at the Great Western Forum. Trailing the Edmonton Oilers 5–0 after two periods, the team that had looked flatter than roadkill, suddenly came to life in the third, counting four unanswered goals during a 13-minute span. Then, with only five seconds left to play, Steve Bozek swiped at a rebound and scored, forcing overtime in Game 3 of a series that no one predicted would be so close. The Oilers, who had amassed a record 48 points more than the lowly Kings during the regular season, figured the best-of-five series would be a cakewalk. But now their confidence had taken a major hit. The resurgent Kings consummated their date with Destiny early in overtime, when the all-rookie trio of Bozek, Doug Smith and Daryl Evans lined up to the left of Grant Fuhr. Smith won the draw, and Evans moved in and slapped the puck high beyond the reach of Fuhr's glove. The Forum crowd roared with delight as Evans was mobbed in celebration. The Kings' six-goal rally became known as the "Miracle on Manchester." Although the feat has occurred during regular-season play, there has never been a greater single-game comeback in Stanley Cup hockey.

THE LONG SHOT

Ron Hextall, Philadelphia Flyers, December 8, 1987

Few netminders ever exhibited greater skill with any piece of equipment than Ron Hextall did with a goalie stick. Some of his peers were masters in the art of the poke-check, the paddle-down save, and the axe-chop, but Hextall redefined the stick's effectiveness through his superiority at puck control. His stick became more than just a defensive weapon for stopping pucks and disciplining opponents. He used it to counterattack on dump-ins, acting as a third defenseman, much as Jacques Plante did decades earlier, but more effectively. Where Plante wandered from his net to make short passes, the ever-mobile Hextall was shooting and lifting the puck to deliver pinpoint breakout passes for the quick turn-around. He was the first NHL goalie with a curved blade. It gave his shot more power. And he perfected his aim by extending the narrow part of his shaft for greater leverage when shooting. He finally made good on his ambitions late in a 4–2 game against Boston. Bruins goalie Réjean Lemelin was pulled and when Gord Kluzak fired wide of the Flyers net, Hextall collected the puck and launched it over everybody. It landed at the Bruins blue line and slid into the vacated net inside the right post. After 70 years and more than 40,000 games, the NHL had its first goal off a netminder's stick. It could only belong to Hextall.

LAST GOAL OF THE ORIGINAL SIX

George Armstrong, Toronto Maple Leafs, May 2, 1967

They could not shoehorn another soul into Maple Leaf Gardens that night in 1967. Programs, now priceless souvenirs, cost $1.25. Scalpers charged $25 for tickets. And "Leafs Nation" was still in its infancy. They came for another Stanley Cup and, as we know, fedora-clad Punch Imlach's over-the-hill gang claimed the silver jug against archrival Montreal in a Game 6 stunner that still reverberates through time. The Cup winner came on a Jim Pappin pass that went in off a skate *(see photo)*. But the truly historic goal was the next one. It ended the wonderfully quaint "Original Six" era, a quarter-century of six-team hockey that iced some of the NHL's greatest stars. However, the six-team era also gave us the modern game; and with its popularity, expansion. The final stroke came on George Armstrong's insurance marker into a vacated Habs net. In the final minute of the 2–1 game and a crucial faceoff in the Leafs zone, who did Imlach send out against the noble Jean Béliveau but 41-year-old clutch-and-grabber Allen Stanley. Of course, Stanley tied up Big Jean and the puck went to Red Kelly, who fed it up to Bob Pulford. A cross-ice pass to Armstrong and the Cup was Toronto's. It remains the Maple Leafs' last sip of glory. Of greater significance, the golden era of hockey was over.

"WE WANT MARCH!"

Mush March, Chicago Blackhawks, April 10, 1934

"A lightweight with the impact of a 10-ton truck against Detroit," was the accolade accorded to Chicago's five-foot-five, 154-pound Mush March during the Blackhawks–Red Wings' struggle for the 1934 Stanley Cup. By Game 4 of the best-of-five final, Chicago held a 2–1 series lead. But regulation and 30 minutes of overtime had settled nothing in a scoreless match that would either hand Detroit crucial momentum for the Cup game or claim the Hawks champion, their first in franchise history. Then, Chicago caught a break with the game's first man-advantage situation. Doc Romnes fed a mid-ice pass to March, who drove up the right boards, tapped the puck away from his check, recovered it and wheeled into Wings territory. Almost hemmed in by defenders, he deked out Walt Buswell and fired a waist-high shot that flashed past Wilf Cude. With their stunning victory, the triumphant Hawks leapt onto the ice in celebration. In what is considered an NHL first, Hawks wingman Louis Trudel "grabbed the Stanley Cup as soon as it was brought on the ice for the presentation and skated wildly around the rink," the *Detroit News* reported. March declined to celebrate but the jubilant Chicago crowd chanted "We want March!" and the reluctant hero of 1934 was persuaded to circle the ice with Trudel under a deafening ovation.

TEEDER TAKES CHARGE

Ted Kennedy, Toronto Maple Leafs, April 19, 1947

Most hockey pundits felt that the defending champion Montreal Canadiens would have little trouble defeating the Toronto Maple Leafs in the 1947 Cup final. The "Leaflets," as the Toronto press dubbed them, had 12 players aged 23 years or younger. This lack of experience looked to be a recipe for failure, especially after the Habs thumped the Leafs 6–0 in Game 1. The contest was so one-sided that Montreal netminder Bill Durnan mockingly asked reporters, "How did those guys get into the playoffs?" Inspired by Durnan's comments, Toronto surprised everyone by winning four of the next five games of a violent and emotionally charged series to claim the Cup. The Leafs' attack was spearheaded by its young line of Ted "Teeder" Kennedy (21), Howie Meeker (22) and Vic Lynn (21), which had its best game of the series in the decisive sixth game. Montreal had taken an early lead, but Lynn tied it up in the second period with assists going to Kennedy and Meeker. Then, in the third, with less than six minutes remaining, Kennedy fired a low drive past Durnan. Despite unleashing a fusillade of shots at the Leaf goal in the final minutes, Montreal could not beat Turk Broda, and so Kennedy, who had scored the winning goal in three of Toronto's four victories, became the youngest player to net a Cup winner.

57

STEVIE WONDER

Steve Yzerman, Detroit Red Wings, February 26, 1989

In 1988–89, Steve Yzerman racked up 65 goals and 90 assists for 155 points. Few remember this amazing performance, however, because Yzerman finished third in the NHL scoring race, 13 behind Wayne Gretzky (168) and a whopping 44 points behind Mario Lemieux (199 points). Playing in the shadow of those two great centres was a major reason why Yzerman was only elected to one All-Star Team in his career. The Detroit captain did, however, score a stunning goal that season during which he made the Chicago Blackhawks look like a crew of drunken sailors. After receiving a pass at his own blue line, Yzerman raced up the left side and penetrated the Chicago zone where he deked defenseman Steve Konroyd and came toward the net. As goalie Darren Pang came out to make a poke-check, Yzerman circled back and then cut toward the centre of the ice. When several Hawks closed that alley, he headed back toward the blue line and made another turn. At this point the two players chasing him peeled off to pick up their checks. Given an open lane, Yzerman accelerated toward the net, shifted around defenseman Keith Brown and fired a shot under the crossbar. All told, Stevie Wonder controlled the puck for 15 seconds without being touched by a Chicago player, before turning on the red light.

THE SEIBERT GOAL

Maurice Richard, Montreal Canadiens, February 3, 1945

During Maurice Richard's record-setting drive to deliver hockey's first 50-goal season in 1944–45, one singular play from that momentous campaign stood out and announced to the world his extraordinary athletic abilities. By January, he had already established his sniper credentials by challenging Joe Malone's regular-season goal mark and brought himself fistic fame for his wild double knockout of Bob "Killer" Dill in New York. Then, in Detroit, he scored his 38th of 1944–45 on a solo effort that became widely known as the "Seibert Goal," and, in some circles, his greatest goal ever. The play developed near the Red Wings blue line where Earl Seibert, a tough, burly 210-pound defenseman, had lowered the boom on Richard. After both men collided, they wobbled for an instant and then regained their balance, only now with Seibert draped all over Richard. Even under that unexpected weight, Richard still managed to recover his speed within three strides. Seibert refused to let go and was carried almost 60 feet by Richard, who never lost control of the puck while fighting off his assailant. Still weighed down, Richard faked out goalie Harry Lumley and with his one free hand on his stick flicked the disk into the net. As he scored, Richard finally shook Seibert free and tossed him into the corner.

CAPPING THE COMEBACK

Ed Westfall, New York Islanders, April 26, 1975

The situation looked grim for the New York Islanders. Down three games to none against the Pittsburgh Penguins in a quarterfinals series in which they had never once even held the lead in a game, the Isles were teetering on the brink of elimination. Only one team in NHL history had managed to claw its way back to win a playoff series after being down by three games: the Toronto Maple Leafs in the 1942 Stanley Cup Final. But that was a battle-hardened team that had competed in three finals in the previous four years. In contrast, the Islanders were in only their third year of existence and were competing in the postseason for the first time. Islanders coach Al Arbour challenged his players prior to Game 4, saying, "If there's anyone here who doesn't feel we can come back and beat these guys, get off the ice immediately." Defying the odds, the underdogs posted three wins straight to send the series back to Steeltown for a Game 7 showdown. Behind Chico Resch's clutch goaltending, the Isles completed the miraculous comeback, winning 1–0 on a goal by captain Ed Westfall, who hit the twine with just over five minutes left in regulation. Amazingly, the never-say-die Islanders almost repeated the feat in their next series, falling behind Philadelphia by three games, then rallying to force a Game 7, before losing 4–1.

SUMMIT SERIES SOLO

Peter Mahovlich, Canada, September 4, 1972

Peter Mahovlich netted 288 NHL goals, but none was prettier, or more inspired, than his lone marker at the legendary Summit Series. In fact, apart from Paul Henderson's dramatic series winner, Mahovlich's shorthanded goal in Game 2 may be the best remembered, both by Canadian and Soviet fans. The play began with Canada up 2–1 but the Russians pressing hard on the power play. Phil Esposito sent a blind clearing pass off the boards and onto the stick of Mahovlich. From his own blue line, Mahovlich gathered steam up ice, deftly swept around Soviet defender Yevgeny Poladiev with a fake slapper and then produced a forehand-backhand deke on Vladislav Tretiak that sent the Russian goalie sprawling and Maple Leafs Gardens into pandemonium. Tretiak couldn't understand his misplay: "Technically, I played it perfectly. And I did not make a mistake. Still, he got the puck past me and scored a very big goal. It was like magic." Mahovlich put Canada up 3–1 and halted a potential Soviet comeback similar to the 7–3 debacle in Montreal two nights earlier. Canada's monumental 4–1 win in Toronto was its only victory on home soil during the series. Today, many consider Mahovlich's highlight-reel special against Tretiak as one of the greatest goals ever scored in international hockey.

JAGRMEISTER

Jaromir Jagr, Pittsburgh Penguins, May 26, 1992

Jaromir Jagr scored a dozen stand-up-and-cheer goals during his NHL career, but the one that best combined athletic artistry and clutch timing was the one that he bagged against Chicago in Game 1 of the 1992 Stanley Cup Final. Although Pittsburgh was the defending champion, many felt that the Blackhawks, who entered the series riding an 11-game winning streak, would take the Cup. The Hawks' hard-nosed checking style and the brilliance of goaltender Ed Belfour were thought to be the ideal antidote to the Penguins' offensive dazzle. When Chicago jumped out to a seemingly invincible 4–1 lead in Game 1, it began to look that way, but Pittsburgh fought back on goals by Rick Tocchet and Mario Lemieux. Then, with about five minutes left to play, Jagr seized the moment. Spinning off the side boards in the Hawks zone, the 20-year-old Czech eluded Brent Sutter, then danced around three more Chicago defenders before whipping a backhand past Belfour. "There are only four people in the rink that he didn't deke and three of those are ushers," exclaimed TV analyst Harry Neale. Four minutes later, with Steve Smith in the penalty box for hooking, Lemieux snapped home a rebound to complete the comeback. The revitalized Penguins went on to win the series in a sweep.

A THAW IN THE ICE AGE

Luc Robitaille, Canada, May 8, 1994

Icing a roster of top-shelf NHLers eliminated from Stanley Cup action, Canada looked to possess the horses to finally break through after 33 years of gold-medal frustration and win the 1994 World Championships. The Canadians, with Joe Sakic, Brendan Shanahan and Rob Blake, scorched everyone in their path, including Sweden in a 6–0 semifinal blowout that earned them a championship match against undefeated Finland. But the Finns led after a third-period goal in the tight 1–0 game. Then, with five minutes left, Rod Brind'Amour pulled Canada even to force overtime. After 10 minutes of OT, nothing was decided, nor after each team scored twice in the first five shootout attempts. At the one-and-one stage, Luc Robitaille got the nod from coach George Kingston. Lucky Luc was hot, after notching an assist on Brind'Amour's regulation marker and one of two shootout goals, only moments earlier. Robitaille skated in slowly on goalie Jarmo Myllys, but midway lost possession of the puck on a rough patch of ice. Within a stride he regained puck control and just in front of Myllys unleashed a masterful backhand that fooled the Finnish netminder. Then, Bill Ranford stopped Mika Nieminen on his effort. Robitaille's dramatic goal ended Canada's 33-year drought in a way no Canadian player wanted—the shootout.

BABE'S BEAUTY

Babe Pratt, Toronto Maple Leafs, April 22, 1945

The Toronto Maple Leafs had little hope of winning the Stanley Cup in 1945. Their semifinal opponents, the Canadiens, had finished with 28 more points in regular-season action; and if Toronto survived Montreal to reach the final it would likely face Detroit, which had lost only one game against the Maple Leafs in their 10 seasonal meetings. But in a playoff round that many Leafs of that era hailed as coach Hap Day's finest, Toronto stunned the 38–8–4 Canadiens with a 4–2 series win. Seemingly, little would be left for the Red Wings, as Leafs star Ted Kennedy assessed, "our tongues were hanging out." However, Day had his outmanned squad playing clutch defense and rookie Frank McCool was on fire in Toronto's nets, blanking the Wings 1–0, 2–0 and 1–0 in the first three games. Fatigue finally took hold as the Leafs dropped the next three, setting up a Game 7 finale and a possible Detroit Cup, which would be huge payback for the Leafs' stunning comeback of 1942 when they won four straight from the Red Wings after a three-game deficit. In a tense 1–1 tie in the third period, a bouncing puck in a goal-mouth scramble at Harry Lumley's crease brought Babe Pratt in on a risky play from the point. Pratt found the puck, fired point-blank to beat Lumley low to score the biggest upset of the six-team era.

A COFFEY BREAK

Mike Bossy, Canada, September 13, 1984

Few individual efforts have altered the course of a championship more dramatically than Paul Coffey's defense manoeuvre against two Soviet attackers during semifinal action at the 1984 Canada Cup. Canada easily held the edge in play, but not on the scoreboard. Tied 2–2, 12 minutes into overtime, Vladimir Kovin and Mikhail Varnakov streaked across Canada's blue line in a lethal two-on-one with only goalie Pete Peeters standing between Coffey and a potential Canada Cup defeat. It should have been textbook for the Russians against Coffey, who was sometimes called "Paul Cough-up" or, as the joke went, a pastry chef for his knack at turnovers. But the Canadian rearguard read Kovin's saucer pass to Varnakov perfectly and lifted his stick at the exact moment to intercept the puck. He quickly counterattacked into the Soviet zone and when the puck went in the corner, John Tonelli dug it out and fed it back to Coffey pinching in from the point. Meanwhile, Mike Bossy had just been knocked down battling with Soviet defenders at the net. He climbed to his feet, got his stick up and managed to deflect Coffey's shot past goalie Vladimir Myshkin. From interception to deflection, the play and goal took 31 seconds and produced the tournament's masterpiece move. Canada won 3–2 and later subdued Sweden in the final.

THE STICK THAT WON THE CUP

Nels Stewart, Montreal Maroons, April 6, 1926

It may be the best hockey stick story in Stanley Cup lore. The Montreal Maroons had just lost Game 3 against the Victoria Cougars in the best-of-five final of 1926. Rookie Nels Stewart was Montreal's scoring ace and the main reason the Maroons were challenging for the Cup. The 23-year-old won the scoring title in 1925–26, the only time a rookie ever did so, and potted four goals in the final's first three games to give Montreal a 2–1 series lead over the Cougars. But Victoria's lone win had spooked Stewart. For the next match, he wanted his stick from the previous round's victory over Ottawa. However, the lumber belonged to a Maroons' fan after Stewart gave it up as a souvenir. After some hasty negotiations, the stick was returned for the key contest against Victoria. Stewart went out with his trusty blade and made the Maroons champions, scoring both goals in the 2–0 Cup victory. The winner came as Montreal swarmed Harry Holmes in a wild goalmouth scramble. After four Maroons shots failed, Stewart sensed his chance and circled behind the net. His strategy caught the desperate Cougar defense by surprise and Holmes couldn't get across in time. Stewart slid the puck home to deliver the Montreal Forum's very first Cup. After the game, the stick was returned, giving the fan a piece of Stanley Cup history.

WHO LET THE DOG OUT?

Rick Nash, Columbus Blue Jackets, January 17, 2008

Rick Nash was in the doghouse—but not for very long. Late in a 2008 game against the Phoenix Coyotes, the Blue Jackets right winger had taken a careless penalty for high-sticking and Phoenix had scored on the ensuing power play to tie the contest 3–3. On the next shift, Nash made amends. He took a long outlet pass from Mike Peca just outside the Phoenix blue line and then turned defensemen Keith Ballard and Derek Morris into pretzels with a rapid series of astonishing dekes, before faking goalie Mikael Tellqvist to the ice and tapping the puck into the net. The highlight-reel marker, scored with only 21 seconds left, lifted Columbus to a fourth straight win. Meanwhile, Nash's remarkable display of soft hands, balance and coordination became an instant Internet sensation. The "goal of the year" as it was called, would later be nominated for an ESPY Award in the category of Best Play. So how is a player who is six-foot-four and 220 pounds able to pull off Houdini-like moves in such close quarters? Instinct, apparently. The Columbus gunner had no clue. "I pretty much blacked out," Nash told reporters. "It just seemed like the puck was on a string. It was amazing how everything went right. It was unbelievable."

Mike Bossy, New York Islanders, January 24, 1981

Thirty-six years, some 12,000 NHL games and no one, not Bobby Hull, Phil Esposito nor Guy Lafleur, had equalled Maurice Richard's 50-goals-in-50-games of 1944–45. No one, until Mike Bossy in 1980–81. The Isles' young winger raised eyebrows around the league when he boldly predicted he would reach the hallowed milestone. Granted, he had three straight 50-goal seasons during his meteoric ascent to NHL superstardom. But 50-in-50? Esposito had kind of done it in 1971–72, when he scored 53 goals in 50 games, but that blitz came at season's end of his 76-goal year. Now Bossy took aim; and, sure enough, his goal-a-game pace stalled at 48 goals by Game 47. He missed two empty-netters in Game 48 and nothing came his way in Game 49, nor through most of Game 50, where he went without a shot in two periods while being double-teamed by the Quebec Nordiques. Suddenly, with four minutes left and on a power play, Bossy backhanded his 49th past goalie Ron Grahame. Then at 18:31, Bryan Trottier fed Bossy a perfect pass. But the puck bounced up. Bossy took a second to lay it flat and buried it on Grahame's short side. Nassau Coliseum erupted. Afterwards, Bossy ribbed Richard. "He'll claim he still holds the record because I scored my 50th in the last minute and he scored his with two minutes to go."

THE MILLENNIUM MARKER

Gordie Howe, New England Whalers, December 7, 1977

Let's face it, hockey's first 1,000th career goal gets no respect. Among the game's greatest milestones, Gordie Howe's millennium marker rarely earns any notice. Given how such standards as the first 50th or 500th goals are revered, certainly, the Howe achievement deserves its due, even though regular-season and playoff goals aren't normally totalled, nor usually combined with rival WHA numbers as career benchmarks. But, at the time, Gordie's pro aggregate was followed closely and his quest for No. 1,000 weighed heavily both on his mind and those of his teammates, after No. 999 came 10 agonizing games earlier. Then, in early December 1977, Birmingham Bulls goalie John Garrett gave up a rebound after New England Whaler Mike Antonovich hit the post with a shot. Johnny McKenzie shovelled the puck at the Bulls goal only to have Garrett kick it out, but right onto the stick of Howe. The 49-year-old Howe had employed every type of shot imaginable in every hockey circumstance possible, but the game's first quadruple-figured goal was scored just like his first goal 31 years earlier: a short wrist shot. Howe, who had an injured wrist, was so focussed, that coach Harry Neale said that between shifts he kept his hand in an ice bucket to numb the pain. Howe later recalled: "I guess I wanted that goal."

THE GREAT UPSET

Howie Morenz, Montreal Canadiens, April 3, 1930

He could do everything. Shoot. Score. Check. But Howie Morenz was really always about speed. He pulled fans out of their seats with his electrifying rink-long rushes. And he scored with amazing consistency, becoming the first true superstar of the NHL and the big reason the Canadiens were nicknamed the "Flying Frenchmen." Montreal was *the* team to beat, while Morenz, the club's centrepiece, was the Wayne Gretzky of his time, selling the game to American audiences. The 1930 Stanley Cup Final featured Morenz's Canadiens against the defending Cup champion Boston Bruins. The Bruins owned 1929–30 with a 38–5–1 record, still the best winning percentage today. They had not lost back-to-back games all season and won all four contests against Montreal. However, the best-of-three final proved a different challenge. Montreal, playing the underdog role, used speed and momentum to its advantage, with a startling 3–0 win in the first game. Game 2 was no different, 3–0, until Eddie Shore scored in the second period to help rally Boston. But before the Bruins could build on it, Morenz got the goal back with a quick shot to the far corner behind Tiny Thompson. It proved to be the Cup winner. Boston's shocking defeat led the league to lengthen the final to a best-of-five series in the future.

THE EASTER EPIC

Pat LaFontaine, New York Islanders, April 18–19, 1987

Whenever fans meet Pat LaFontaine, they still remind him of the "Easter Epic." They never forgot his famous goal, the one that ended the longest Game 7 in NHL history. It came in 1987's first playoff round between two teams looking to shake off their mantle of mediocrity: the former powerhouse Islanders and perennial choker Washington Capitals. New York was facing a long summer of regret, but battled back with consecutive wins to force the seventh and deciding game. Nothing was settled in regulation and the punishing 3–3 deadlock went into overtime. And several more overtimes. Then, eight minutes into the fourth extra period, the Islanders' Gord Dineen skated in and around goalie Bob Mason and fired at the net. The shot, blocked by Kevin Hatcher, came out near the Capitals blue line. LaFontaine picked up the deflected puck as it was rolling on edge. He spun around and drilled it through a maze of bodies. The shot streaked past Rod Langway and several other players without changing direction and into the net beyond Mason. The Washington crowd fell silent as the young centre was smothered. "It was the most memorable moment in my hockey life," LaFontaine later said. His dramatic winner came on the game's 130th shot, just before 2:00 AM on April 19th, Easter Sunday.

71

THE HISTORY MAKER

Maurice Richard, Montreal Canadiens, November 8, 1952

When Maurice Richard scored a goal at the Montreal Forum, it was said that the ensuing thunder represented something more that a change in the score. The Forum faithful were cheering for the man himself, but also, in some deeper way, because of their connection to him, for their own game in life. Each fed off the other, too. The chants became battle cries to the warrior in Richard and, accordingly, he rarely played as great away as on home ice. After tying Nels Stewart's career mark of 324 goals, he waited three games to pocket the all-time record 325th. By that time, Canadiens fans were "intoxicated with tension," as the *Montreal Star* noted. In a way, it became their record as much as his. In front of 14,562 fans, Richard parlayed a Butch Bouchard pass to break in on Chicago goalie Al Rollins. He fired a low backhander from about 20 feet out that Rollins fumbled trying to trap. As Bert Olmstead desperately stabbed to jam the puck home, it trickled through and into hockey immortality. Some say Olmstead touched the puck last, but referee Red Storey pointed at Richard. The Forum shook as flashbulbs popped and game programs showered down. Play was halted for Richard to recover the puck. It was later gold-plated and sent to Her Majesty Queen Elizabeth at Buckingham Palace, where it still resides today.

TOP SHELF

Steve Yzerman, Detroit Red Wings, May 16, 1996

Of all the 807 regular-season and playoff goals that Steve Yzerman scored in his storied NHL career, his personal favourite came in 1996. Even though it didn't win a Stanley Cup, it was a critical goal in Red Wings history. It won a playoff series against a hated division rival, in Game 7, in double overtime, and lifted a huge millstone from Yzerman's neck. Although no one questioned Yzerman's talent, the team he had captained for nine years had repeatedly tanked in the postseason. In 1995–96, Detroit won an NHL-record 62 games and was expected to cruise to the Cup final. But after defeating the St. Louis Blues convincingly in the first two games of the conference finals, Detroit lost three in a row and looked to be on the verge of a devastating choke. The Wings eked out a 4–2 road victory in Game 6, but Game 7 was a nail-biter. The score remained tied 0–0 through 60 minutes and one overtime period, with the Blues' Jon Casey and Detroit's Chris Osgood trading clutch saves. Then at 1:15 of double overtime, Yzerman ripped a sudden slapshot from just inside the blue line that hit the back of the net over the shoulder of a stunned Casey. Joe Louis Arena erupted, the Red Wings bench emptied and Yzerman, who had just posted his first overtime playoff goal, was crushed under a pile of joyful teammates.

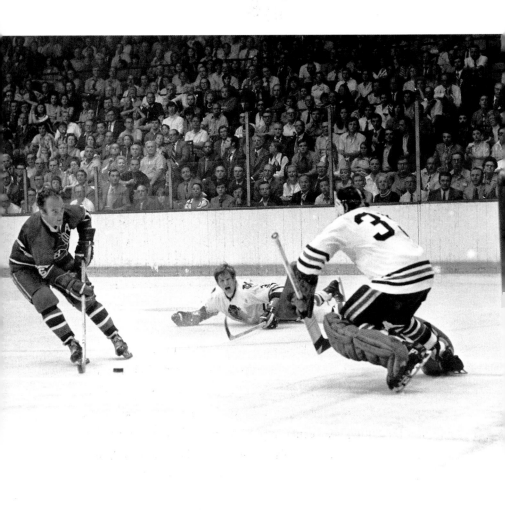

73

RICHARD TO THE RESCUE

Henri Richard, Montreal Canadiens, May 18, 1971

Rookie goalie Ken Dryden and veterans Frank Mahovlich and Jean Béliveau sparked the Montreal Canadiens to a huge upset over the defending champion Boston Bruins in the first round of the 1971 play-offs, but in the Cup final versus a powerful Chicago Blackhawks squad, the guy who put the Habs over the top was little Henri Richard. The centre had actually been benched in Game 5 of the series by rookie coach Al MacNeil, a decision that prompted an irate Richard to declare to reporters, "He's the worst coach I ever played for." If MacNeil's plan had been to light a fire under the "Pocket Rocket," it certainly worked, as Richard turned in what may have been the finest performance of his career in Game 7. After Jacques Lemaire beat Chicago netminder Tony Esposito with a long slapshot to trim Chicago's lead to 2–1 in the second period, Richard took over. Four minutes later, he tied the game, converting a pass from Lemaire. Then, early in the third, Richard struck again, taking a pass from Réjean Houle and waltzing around defenseman Keith Magnuson. Cutting in alone on Esposito, he flipped a wrist shot over the falling goalkeeper to put Montreal ahead for good. Afterwards, as he drank champagne from the Cup in the Montreal dressing room, Richard called it, "The best of the 10 Cups I've won."

MAD MAX: ROAD WARRIOR

Maxime Talbot, Pittsburgh Penguins, June 12, 2009

The Pittsburgh Penguins were not supposed to win the Stanley Cup in 2009, not with rookie coach Dan Bylsma calling the shots. They were not supposed to deep-six the defending champion Detroit Red Wings in the final either, especially after falling behind three games to one. And they were not supposed to win Game 7 at Detroit's Joe Louis Arena with star centre Sidney Crosby limping and leading scorer Evgeni Malkin unable to find any open ice. But strange things often happen when it's all on the line. In this case, the strange thing that happened was winger Maxime Talbot, the 234th pick in the 2002 Entry Draft, and a guy who had never scored more than 13 goals in a season, suddenly making like Mario Lemieux and notching both of Pittsburgh's goals in a thrilling 2–1 victory. Both came in the second period, the first after Brad Stuart's outlet pass deflected directly to Talbot, who slid a shot between Chris Osgood's pads. He scored his second at 10:07, wiring a shot over Osgood's outstretched trapper. It proved to be the difference. Detroit's Jonathan Ericsson got one back in the third, but the Wings could not beat netminder Marc-André Fleury again. And so the Penguins became the first team in 38 years to win a Game 7 in the final on the road, and Talbot became an overnight folk hero.

INDEPENDENCE GOAL

Peter Bondra, Slovakia, May 11, 2002

Peter Bondra's stunning goal with 100 seconds left at the 2002 World Championships represented much more than a gold-medal victory for tiny Slovakia. It was as if independence from Czechoslovakia had been declared all over again. The stirring 4–3 win against Russia not only validated its hockey program, but its sovereignty as an independent country. Only eight years earlier the famed Czechoslovak hockey system had been dissolved, with the Czech Republic keeping its position of former Czechoslovakia and the Slovaks becoming a new hockey nation in the IIHF pool rankings. As a result, Slovakia started in lowly Pool C in 1994. However, it quickly rose through the divisions and in 2002 made history on Bondra's gold-medal winner. The score was tied 3–3 and overtime against Russia seemed inevitable, when Ziggy Palffy fed a seeing-eye pass to Bondra streaking in on the left wing. From near the faceoff dot, the Ukrainian-born sniper unleashed a blast at Maxim Sokolov that sneaked by the goalie's attempted kick save, struck the inside post and ricocheted into the net. Following the victory, players kissed the Scandinavian ice and back home millions of fans set off a national frenzy. More importantly, Slovakia had established itself as an international force to challenge the top six hockey nations.

THE KILLER INSTINCT

Doug Gilmour, Toronto Maple Leafs, May 3, 1993

Doug "Killer" Gilmour was arguably the best player on the first two NHL teams he played for—the St. Louis Blues and Calgary Flames—but was never regarded as the go-to-guy in either of those places. It was not until after Gilmour was traded to Toronto midway through the 1991–92 campaign that the hockey world began to truly appreciate his gifts. As teammate Dave Andreychuk noted: "I've played with bigger players and maybe more talented players, but to me this is a guy that did everything he could to make the team win and to make people around him better. There was nobody better at that, that I've ever played with." Of all the big goals that Gilmour scored for the Leafs, it is his double-overtime goal against the Blues in Game 1 of the 1993 division finals for which he is most remembered. Only 48 hours after eliminating Detroit in a gruelling seven-game series, Toronto was now locked in a titanic struggle against the well-rested Blues. The 1–1 game went to the fourth minute of the second overtime before Gilmour found himself with the puck behind the Blues net and goalie Curtis Joseph, who had played magnificently, having withstood a barrage of 63 shots. Gilmour juked back and forth, confusing both the St. Louis defense and Joseph, before finally tucking the winner inside the post on his backhand. Game over.

WILLIE'S TIME

Willie O'Ree, Boston Bruins, January 1, 1961

While Willie O'Ree is the first black to play in the NHL, he never influenced his sport to the degree Jackie Robinson did with baseball. O'Ree, for all his on-ice skill, was simply the first. And although he faced racial abuse throughout his career, unlike Robinson, who integrated major league baseball, O'Ree's historic appearance was short-lived and drew almost no media attention in January 1958. As he said years later: "There wasn't much of a big thing made of it in the papers the next day." Still, his debut was a courageous act, and happened long before another black athlete played in the league in 1974. Unfortunately, O'Ree, at 22, managed only one more match before his return to the minors, which is where he spent most of his career except for another NHL stint in 1960–61. This time he stayed 43 games with the Bruins and scored on New Year's Day 1961 at Boston Garden. It came against Montreal halfway through the third period after O'Ree took a pass from Leo Boivin. In full stride, streaking down left wing, he accelerated and cut in around one rearguard, deked behind the last defender back and found himself in alone on goalie Charlie Hodge. O'Ree shot low along the ice against Hodge. The puck struck the inside left post and went in. The colour barrier in hockey had officially been broken.

MOTOWN MAGICIAN

Steve Yzerman, Detroit Red Wings, November 12, 1998

There are not many players who can make other NHL pros look like they are moving in slow motion. But Steve Yzerman was one of those guys. In the years before he suffered serious knee injuries and became better known for his stellar two-way play and leadership qualities, Yzerman was one of the league's most electrifying offensive threats, someone who could create spectacular goals all by himself. In 1988–89, Yzerman lit it up like never before, compiling 155 points, a total only ever exceeded by Wayne Gretzky and Mario Lemieux. In November of that banner season, he began what would become a career-high 28-game scoring streak. During the streak, the Red Wings captain scored a spectacular goal in a 5–4 win over Philadelphia that began as Yzerman picked up the puck at his own blue line and steamed toward the Flyers zone. He dodged two defenders at the blue line, leaping to avoid a cross-check and still stay onside, as the Flyers defenders forced him to the centre of the ice. Wheeling sharply, he shed a backchecking forward, dismissively sidestepped the lone remaining defenseman and completely undressed goalie Ron Hextall, before putting the puck into the vacant net on Hextall's stick side. All of this was done at warp speed and without any wasted motion or hesitation. It was Yzerman eye candy at its finest.

THE SULTAN OF SLOT

Phil Esposito, Boston Bruins, March 2, 1969

They didn't stop cheering for 10 minutes, as the capacity crowd of 14,659 fans littered hats, programs and other debris onto the Boston Garden ice. The joyful delirium was for Phil Esposito and the goal against Pittsburgh that brought him one of hockey's greatest milestones: the first 100-point season in NHL history. It came just one day after Esposito thrilled the Garden crowd with his record 98th point, which topped Bobby Hull's league mark of 97 in 1965–66. Esposito always had impeccable timing, particularly around the net. But to break Hull's league record and then score the milestone point, in back-to-back home games on consecutive nights, well, that was nothing short of spine-tingling. It could not have been better scripted, even the goal itself, which came on a third-period rush by linemate Ken Hodge, who carried the puck deep into opposing territory, controlling it until Esposito could set himself up in the slot. This time, Espo took Hodge's lead pass just to the left before jamming it under goalie Joe Daley. Then a roar like a freight train descended from the rafters. It drowned out Frank Fallon's announcement of the goal and in the chaos a chant began: "We want Espo!" The man took a short skate to centre ice, acknowledged the crowd and, later, scored another goal to put an exclamation point on the evening.

SMOKIN' THE SOVIETS

Norm Lenardon, Canada, March 12, 1961

By some fan accounts, Norm Lenardon's dramatic goal at the 1961 World Championships was Paul Henderson-like in its late heroics for Canada. Similar to Henderson's famous 1972 tally, the Lenardon theatrics came against the Soviet Union, but under far different circumstances. In 1961, Canada was represented by the Trail Smoke Eaters, an amateur team locked in a three-way gold-medal race against Czechoslovakia and the Soviets. Each country had emerged as a rival to Canada's supremacy on the world stage; and now the Czechs were poised to embarrass the Canadians at their own game. They beat the Soviets 6–4 and knotted the Smokies 1–1 to equal Canada in the standings. In the final match against Russia, Canada had to win by four goals to finish ahead of the Czechs. Canada dominated the play but victory only came with two minutes left when Lenardon stripped the puck from defenseman Nikolai Sologubov. Off-balance, he slapped it high into the net for the 5–1 win. The right winger went sprawling on the ice and was mobbed by teammates, including goalie Seth Martin, who skated the length of the rink for the pile-on. At the game's conclusion, Lenardon was carried from the ice by cheering players. The Smokies were the last amateur team to win a World Championship for Canada.

THE GHOSTBUSTER

Doug Gilmour, Calgary Flames, May 25, 1989

No team had ever captured the Stanley Cup by beating the Montreal Canadiens at the Montreal Forum. Whatever mysterious mojo the "Flying Frenchmen" had on their side, the hex had held sway for 65 years. But this would change in 1989. The Cup final pitted Calgary and Montreal in a rematch of their 1986 showdown, which Montreal won in five games. The 1989 series saw the teams split the first four games. Calgary then grabbed the edge with a 3–2 win on home ice in Game 5. Back in the fabled Forum with the 23 Cup banners hanging above, the Habs needed to win to force a Game 7. The Flames snagged a 2–1 lead early in the second period on a goal by 36-year-old Lanny McDonald, and then extended that margin to 3–1 midway through the third, when Doug Gilmour took a pass at full gallop and let fly with a backhander. Patrick Roy stopped the shot, but Gilmour alertly batted the rebound between Roy's pads. Although Rick Green replied for Montreal 51 seconds later, Calgary goalie Mike Vernon turned aside everything else that came his way. Montreal coach Pat Burns pulled Roy for an extra attacker to try to notch the equalizer, but Gilmour took a pass from Al MacInnis, deked around Chris Chelios and coolly fired the puck into the empty cage at 18:57.

GENO'S SPECIAL

Evgeni Malkin, Pittsburgh Penguins, May 21, 2009

It was a command performance worthy of the 2009 Conn Smythe Trophy for 22-year-old Evgeni Malkin, the youngest forward ever named playoff MVP. Malkin, better known to teammates as "Geno," found a way to score against almost every line, regardless of the matchup. He led all post-season scorers but his most inspired play came against Carolina's Cam Ward during Game 2 of the Conference Finals. After winning a draw in the Hurricanes faceoff circle, Malkin pushed the puck forward, regained possession and whipped around Ward's net. On his back, hanging over him like a cheap coat, was Dennis Seidenberg. Ward moved across to block the wraparound, but Malkin skated out from behind the net and curled tight to the post. Seidenberg's stick was to the inside of the play to prevent a Malkin shot from the slot—a normal cover manoeuvre. But the wily centre shifted weight, pivoted and cut sharp away to the outside, making Seidenberg the screen man to his own goalie. With his back to the net, Malkin backhanded a blind riser that must have had GPS functions on board to locate the opening between Ward's shoulder and the crossbar. In slo-mo, Malkin cradled the puck for an instant before shooting, but in real time everyone was left wondering: "How did he score that?"

THE GOLDEN FINNISH

Ville Peltonen, Finland, May 7, 1995

Few World Championships have been as sweet for the home country as Finland's run for the gold in 1995. After two decades on the world stage and many frustrating seasons of near-triumphs, the Finns finally put something together at the 1994 Lillehammer Olympics when they assembled a team around the kid line of Saku Koivu, Ville Peltonen and Jere Lehtinen. Soon, they were dubbed the "Donald Duck Line" and nicknamed Tupu, Hupu and Lupu—Finnish for Uncle Donald's nephew triplets Huey, Dewey and Louie. The threesome clicked but Finland only won Olympic bronze and, later, silver at the 1994 Worlds. The next year, the trio was reunited at the Worlds in Stockholm, where a gold-medal berth was secured against archrival Sweden. Finland beat its Nordic neighbour 4–1 on a hat trick by Peltonen, whose third goal was the Swedish backbreaker. Peltonen, Koivu and defenseman Mika Strömberg set up a perfect tic-tac-toe combination with Koivu dropping the puck back to Strömberg who fed it to Peltonen who found the top shelf behind goalie Thomas Östlund. The Finns won their first-ever world title on their chief adversary's home ice, and with Swedish coach Curt Lindström behind their bench. The victory set off a national frenzy that lasted several days.

LUCKY DEVIL

Jason Arnott, New Jersey Devils, June 10, 2000

The Devil was given a reprieve. Late in the first overtime period of Game 6 of the Stanley Cup Final, Jason Arnott was penalized for delivering a cross-check to the neck of Dallas' Blake Sloan as the forward lay on the ice. It was a nasty foul anytime, but made worse in this case because Sloan was wearing a football-style faceguard to protect two metal plates in the jaw that he broke in February. The infraction could have easily earned the New Jersey centre a major and a game misconduct. As it was, he only received a minor and New Jersey's crack penalty-killing unit held the Stars off the board, preserving the 1–1 tie and saving Arnott from having his name added to the list of playoff goats. The hard-hitting marathon continued into the second overtime with Martin Brodeur and Ed Belfour displaying the same sensational netminding that had extended Game 5 of the series into triple overtime. Then just past the eight-minute mark, with New Jersey back at full strength, Scott Stevens sent the rubber skimming around the boards to the far corner of the Dallas zone. New Jersey's crafty winger Patrik Elias beat everyone to the puck and whipped a hard backhand pass out in front to the left of Belfour. The puck came directly to Arnott, who banged home a one-timer to give the Devils the Cup.

HIGH-FLYING HAWK

Jonathan Toews, Chicago Blackhawks, October 19, 2007

The recent revival of the Chicago Blackhawks franchise officially began on June 24, 2006, when the club selected Jonathan Toews third overall in the NHL Entry Draft. The former US collegiate star began his NHL career with a bang, scoring on his first shot in his first game on October 10, 2006 against San Jose. Toews then proceeded to register a point in each of his first 10 games to compile the second-longest point-scoring streak from the start of an NHL career. But it was his second NHL goal that left Chicago fans agog. In the first period of a scoreless game against the Colorado Avalanche, Toews took a pass in full stride at centre ice and sliced between Milan Hejduk and Scott Hannan into the Colorado zone. Moving at top speed, he then deked defenseman Brett Clark out of his drawers before dancing past goalie José Théodore and depositing the puck into the net. Even in the slo-mo replay, the rookie's rapid-fire moves were hard to follow. "It happened so fast," said Toews. "I was lucky their D-men were a little flatfooted. I don't think they expected me to come in with that much speed. I was pretty pumped." Chicago coach, Denis Savard, who has more than passing familiarity with highlight reel goals, was duly impressed. "We haven't seen a goal like this in a long time," said Savard.

THE ROADRUNNER

Yvan Cournoyer, Montreal Canadiens, May 10, 1973

Explosive speed, a booming shot, stickhandling skill and hockey smarts: Yvan Cournoyer was the total package. All the "Roadrunner" lacked was size, but he more than compensated for his five-foot-seven, 172-pound frame with a burning desire to win. Cournoyer captured 10 Stanley Cups during his career, but the one for which he is most remembered came in 1973, when he set a new NHL mark for playoff goals with 15 and led all scorers with 25 points. Fittingly, the goal that earned him the record was also the Cup winner. It came with the score tied 4–4 and just seconds after a verbal exchange with Chicago's Jerry "King Kong" Korab, as they lined up for a third-period faceoff. "Hey, you little frog," Korab snarled, "What are you going to be when you grow up?" "Something you'll never be," Cournoyer replied, "a goal scorer." Jacques Lemaire broke away with the puck after the draw with Cournoyer on his wing. When Lemaire fired a shot that went high and rebounded off the glass in front of the Chicago net, Cournoyer nimbly slipped around Korab and backhanded the biscuit past goalie Tony Esposito. Then, before the bewildered Blackhawks could recover, Cournoyer set up Marc Tardif for an insurance marker as Montreal won 6–4 and triumphantly raised the Cup on Chicago ice.

SHOOTOUT AT MSG

Marek Malik, New York Rangers, November 26, 2005

By the time the red light flashed a final time in the November 2005 game at Madison Square Garden, rookie netminder Henrik Lundqvist and counterpart Olaf Kolzig had gone head-to-head through regulation, overtime and a record-setting marathon shootout of 15 rounds. Each goalie stopped everything but three goals in 14 rounds with the Rangers' Michael Nylander, Ville Nieminen and Jason Strudwick countering tallies by Washington's Andrew Cassels, Brian Willsie and Bryan Muir. Then, in the 15th round, after the Caps' Matt Bradley wrist shot faltered, defenseman Marek Malik fooled Kolzig on a trick shot with his stick between his skates. "I was watching everything before me," said Malik, the third-to-last shooter available on the Ranger bench. "Olie was unbelievable. He stopped everything, from shots, moves. I just thought to myself, 'Maybe I'll surprise him.'" Not a noted sniper, Malik moved to his right in the slot area, pulled Kolzig with him and then slipped the puck and stick blade back between his legs and shot it into the left corner. "You have to have guts to do that move," said Jaromir Jagr. "In front of 20,000 people watching you, it's not that easy to do." Later, losing goalie Kolzig said: "On this stage, Madison Square Garden, Saturday night... I didn't expect Malik to pull off a move like that."

Darren McCarty, Detroit Red Wings, June 7, 1997

After a 42-year wait, the Stanley Cup finally returned to Hockeytown. The 1997 final showcased Detroit's domination, as the Motown mob outscored the Philadelphia Flyers 16–6 in a four-game sweep. Goalie Mike Vernon was tremendous throughout the playoffs, posting a 1.76 goals-against average and earning MVP honours, but it was hard-rock Wings forward Darren McCarty who stole the show in the second period of Game 4. With the Flyers trailing 1–0 and carrying the play, McCarty delivered the knockout blow, taking the puck at centre, deking defenseman Janne Niinimaa with an inside-out move and eluding goalie Ron Hextall's poke-check to score the prettiest goal of the playoffs. McCarty's masterpiece stood up as the Cup winner in a 2–1 Wings triumph. It was only fitting that McCarty should score the playoff's most memorable goal because he had played a pivotal role in the defining moment of Detroit's season. On March 26, McCarty had punched out Colorado's Claude Lemieux to avenge a controversial hit by Lemieux on Red Wings' Kris Draper from the previous year, and then scored the winning goal in overtime of the brawl-filled game. It was "the game that brought the Red Wings together," said Vernon.

THE KRAUT LINE'S LAST HURRAH

Milt Schmidt, Boston Bruins, March 18, 1952

Milt Schmidt's 200th NHL goal was definitely magical. On the night he scored it against Chicago, Schmidt and his two long-time wingers, Woody Dumart and Bobby Bauer, reunited for one final time. Nick-named the "Kraut Line" because all three players were of Germanic descent, the combo had terrorized opponents in the late 1930s and early 1940s. The line dissolved when Bauer retired in 1947, but when he heard that Dumart and Schmidt were being honoured, Bauer agreed to take part in the festivities. In pre-game ceremonies, the trio was presented with gold watches, silver services and assorted other gifts. Although out of shape, Bauer showed flashes of his former brilliance. In the second period, he fed a pass to Dumart at centre ice. The winger skated in and fired a shot on goal. The rebound came just outside the crease and Schmidt pounced on the puck and drove it into the net past Chicago goalie Harry Lumley. It was the Boston captain's 200th career goal and, appropriately, earned with the linemates with whom he had enjoyed his most glorious moments. Boston's infamous fans, the Gallery Gods, roared like they hadn't in years. Bauer later scored a goal of his own in his last NHL game, and Schmidt collected four points as the Bruins clinched a playoff berth with a 4–0 victory.

THE LACROSSE GOAL

Mike Legg, University of Michigan, March 24, 1996

You just have to see it to believe it. During the 1996 NCAA quarter-finals, Michigan Wolverines centre Mike Legg scored using a manoeuvre never seen in hockey, but well known to its sister sport, lacrosse. In the second period, Legg found himself alone behind the Minnesota net with a loose puck and no one between him and Gophers goalie Steve DeBus. In a moment that stunned hockey fans, Legg scooped up the puck on his stick, twirled it like a lacrosse stick with a motion that had the disk magically stuck to his blade and whirled around the net before whipping it under the crossbar. DeBus stood there bewildered by the move—one that Legg had picked up at minor-leaguer Bill Armstrong's hockey school during the off-season. The play became an Internet hit and earned him several "play of the year" accolades. But the greatest praise came from Sidney Crosby, who imitated Legg with his own lacrosse goal eight years later in the QMJHL. So how does a puck stick on a blade while facing the ice without falling? According to physicists, it works when acceleration is greater than gravity, similar to spinning a half-filled bucket of water over your head. The Wolverines went on to win the national championship, yet one question persists: how long before the trick makes its NHL debut?

THEO'S JOY RIDE

Theoren Fleury, Calgary Flames, April 14, 1991

The 1991 edition of the Battle of Alberta may have been the most savagely contested of all the playoff series in the bitter rivalry between the Edmonton Oilers and the Calgary Flames. Although the high-scoring Flames were favoured to win the Smythe Division semifinals, they found themselves trailing three games to two entering Game 6 at Northlands Coliseum. After falling behind 1–0, Calgary dominated the action but was able to get only one puck past Grant Fuhr, who was at his acrobatic best in the Oilers net. The end to the drama came at 4:40 of overtime when Theo Fleury intercepted a pass, scooted into the Oilers zone, deked Fuhr to the ice and slid a backhand between his pads for the game-winner. Yet even more memorable than the winning goal was Fleury's impromptu celebration, which is now regarded as an iconic moment in Canadian hockey lore. The tiny forward dashed joyfully back down the ice with the entire Flames team in pursuit, before falling to his knees and sliding end over end into the boards where he was submerged beneath a pile of red-shirted bodies. Unfortunately for the Flames, they failed to finish off the Oilers back at home in Game 7, blowing a three-goal lead and losing 5–4 in overtime. Devastated by the defeat, Fleury went on a five-day cocaine and booze binge.

MONDAY NIGHT MIRACLE

Doug Wickenheiser, St. Louis Blues, May 12, 1986

If, as the sports adage goes, the toughest game to win is the one that eliminates your opponent from the playoffs, then the toughest team to beat in that situation may be a Cinderella team. Just ask Minnesota, Toronto and Calgary who all faced St. Louis during its fairy-tale playoff run of 1986. With the Blues icing a roster of rejects cast largely from trades and free agent signings, and a Stanley Cup finalist berth on the line, at some point it was inevitable: the miracle comeback. It began against Minnesota, when St. Louis, down 2–0 in the fifth and final game, clawed out a 6–3 win. Then, the Blues upset Toronto in pivotal Game 5 and won the round after trailing the series 2–1. Next, came Calgary, a superior club that had the series all but won in Game 6, but saw 4–1 and 5–2 leads vanish in the final 12 minutes. St. Louis scored three goals to knot the score 5–5. In overtime, it was Bernie Federko to a streaking Mark Hunter, and when Mike Vernon made the pad save off Hunter, Doug Wickenheiser, who epitomized the team's never-say-die character, was there on Vernon's doorstep to slap in the rebound amid the deafening din of St. Louis Arena. Sadly, in Game 7, the Blues' magic deserted them and they lost 2–1. Wickenheiser summed up the Blues' gallant postseason best: "We just ran out of time."

A FLASH OF RED

William "Flash" Hollett, Detroit Red Wings, March 17, 1945

The great Bobby Orr may have introduced hockey to its greatest oxymoron: the offensive defenseman, but there was another group of intrepid rearguards who preceded No. 4 with skills that surpassed standard blue line positional play. Defensive stalwarts such as Doug Harvey and Tim Horton could do more than just take care of their own end; they also controlled the flow and tempo of the game, led headlong rushes through traffic and delivered pinpoint passes. But, despite such a skill set on the attack, these Original Six giants never played Orr's game-breaking brand of hockey. That job description better suited Flash Hollett, who not only brought superb rushing and stickhandling to the position, but a scorer's touch as well. When 1944–45's First All-Star Team was named, the only spot *not* filled by a Montreal Canadien was Hollett's on defense, a berth secured after a scintillating 20-goal season— the first ever by a blueliner and the gold standard among rearguards today. On rare occasions he replaced an injured forward or fronted the penalty kill, but he was primarily a defenseman; and the first true rushing D-man of the NHL. Hollett's historic 20th came on March 17 in a 4–3 win against Toronto. His mark stood for 24 years, only broken by Orr with 21 goals in 1968–69. Orr needed 67 games; Hollett just 50.

DATSYUK'S DAZZLER

Pavel Datsyuk, Detroit Red Wings, January 3, 2009

From the moment puck and stick made contact at centre ice to the red light blink, it was a masterpiece of puck finesse over 89 feet of ice that simply defied the fundamentals of hockey. When Pavel Datsyuk tried it against Minnesota's Josh Harding in a January 2009 shootout, the four-second dance between player and goalie was truly thrilling. Datsyuk began his acceleration, cutting several quick strides to bear down hard on Harding. Twenty-five feet out: Datsyuk planted both feet square to the goalie to ready his shot. The puck darted back-and-forth in a blur of blade acrobatics. In one fluid motion he pulled the puck back as if to shoot—gave some head fake with a glance to Harding's trapper side. Twelve feet out: Harding committed. And down he went, sliding away, pads splayed out, his catcher ready for the shot that never came. Nine feet out: Datsyuk hung up Harding, who, by now struggled in a vain attempt to cover whatever net he could. Six feet out: Datsyuk set up his most dazzling piece of stick work. He dangled the puck, now slightly behind and away from him; then, flicked it in a backhand pass to *himself*, collected it instantly and lifted his right leg to build torque for his shot. He fired into the near side of the net as Harding, way out of position, attempted a pad save. Humble pie, anyone?

DYNASTY KILLER

Murray Balfour, Chicago Blackhawks, March 26, 1961

The goal didn't clinch a playoff series or win the Stanley Cup, but when Chicago's Murray Balfour scored in triple overtime against Montreal in 1961, the Blackhawks knew that the defending champion Canadiens could be beaten. Chicago had not seen a championship since 1938, and while Montreal had gorged itself on five straight titles from 1956 to 1960, the Habs took nothing for granted under coach Toe Blake. If they were going to lose, it wouldn't be due to complacency. After splitting the first two games of the best-of-seven semifinals, each team played a close-checking Game 3, that left the score tied 1–1 through three periods. In sudden-death overtime, several players hit posts, which extended the match until midway through the third overtime when referee Dalton McArthur handed out a tripping penalty to Dickie Moore. Chicago's power play unit almost immediately set in motion Balfour's goal. Playing point, Stan Mikita half-fanned on a shot that found Balfour by the net. He wheeled around with a backhand shot that went through Jacques Plante's five-hole. After the game, an incensed Blake threw a punch at McArthur, earning himself a league-record $2,000 fine. Montreal won the next game on fumes, but then succumbed to two 3–0 shutouts, ending hockey's greatest string of Stanley Cups.

AMERICA'S FORGOTTEN HERO

John Garrison, USA, February 26, 1933

John Garrison may be the least recognized hockey hero in American sports history. While his name resides among the elite in the US Hockey Hall of Fame, unlike Mike Eruzione, Brett Hull or the Christian brothers, few know of his on-ice accomplishments at the international level. During the 1930s, Garrison was one of the best amateur players and starred, both as a forward and defenseman, on several clubs that won US national titles. The Harvard standout captured a silver medal at the 1932 Winter Games and captained his team to Olympic bronze in 1936 with multiple-goal performances. But his finest hour came with USA's Massachusetts Rangers in the final game of the 1933 World Championships at Zimni Stadion in Prague, Czechoslovakia, when he beat goalie Ron Geddes with a sparkling solo effort that broke a 1–1 regulation tie in overtime against powerful Canada. Garrison's dramatic, unassisted goal, which is almost totally forgotten today, gave USA its first World Championship gold and, 77 years later, it remains the only men's senior Worlds title claimed by an American squad. The stunning 2–1 upset abruptly ended Canada's unbeaten streak of six straight Olympic and World golds and the Toronto Sea Fleas—coached by Harold Ballard— became the first Canadian national team to lose an international game.

MR. CLUTCH

Joe Sakic, Colorado Avalanche, May 8, 1996

Overtime playoff goals are not easy to come by. For example, Gordie Howe, Mario Lemieux and Mark Messier, three legends of the game, never scored an overtime playoff goal. But Joe Sakic scored a record eight of them, which is why "Burnaby Joe" was regarded as such a clutch performer. Of the eight, it is difficult to pick one that stands above the others—after all, they were all big goals. But after careful deliberation the nod goes to Sakic's triple-overtime winner against Chicago in the second round of the 1996 playoffs. This six-game series was a viciously contested affair, featuring bone-rattling hits, superb goaltending and four overtimes. The turning point came in Game 4: Colorado was down 2–1 in the series, playing in Chicago, and would have to win three straight if it lost this game, which was tied 2–2 after regulation. Colorado got the break it needed when Chicago took a penalty in the third overtime. On the resulting power play, Sakic redirected Alexei Gusarov's hard pass past goalie Ed Belfour, who had been virtually unbeatable to that point. After that goal Colorado never looked back and went 10–2 the rest of the playoffs en route to capturing its first Stanley Cup. Sakic led all playoff scorers with 18 goals and 16 assists, including six game-winners and took home the Conn Smythe Trophy as playoff MVP.

BETTER THAN BOLSHOI

Valeri Kamensky, Colorado Avalanche, January 20, 1997

Although it was scored eight years before YouTube launched its video-sharing site in 2005, Valeri Kamensky's spectacular goal against Florida's John Vanbiesbrouck was clearly a product meant for the viral age. Today, more than 12 years later, it still ranks among the most popular goals viewed by fans of the online source. Colorado led 3–2 with about two minutes remaining when Alexei Gusarov flipped a saucer pass to Kamensky, who was flying through the slot from Vanbiesbrouck's stick side. Defenseman Gord Murphy tried to deflect the pass away, and may have got a piece of it, but the puck ended up hitting Kamensky's forward skate blade. It's clear by Kamensky's foot movement that he tapped the puck purposely to position it for a shot. Now he just had to figure how to shoot it, as it danced between his skates. Beezer followed the play perfectly in front of him, but what Kamensky did next, he did on pure instinct. He brought his stick back and tucked it between his legs to fire a backhanded shot blindly at the net. But in order to get enough wood on the puck, Kamensky had to rotate his body with such momentum that after the shot he barrel-rolled 360 degrees through midair. It was classic Bolshoi. Vanbiesbrouck went down squeezing his pads, but the puck sailed through the five-hole for the score. Scary.

THE FIRST ONE

Barney Holden, Portage Lakers, December 9, 1904

Little is known about the very first goal in pro hockey, except that it was scored by Barney Holden, a tough, bruising Manitoba cover point—or defenseman—who was recruited by entrepreneurs from the International Hockey League in 1904–05. At the time, hockey was still amateur, played for the love of the game without compensation. The IHL changed all that when it became the world's first pro league and stocked its rosters with restless players looking to make money in a fledging five-team circuit in Michigan, Pennsylvania and Ontario. The migration of Canuck talent to a mostly US league was nothing short of revolutionary for a sport that obliged its members to play for free. Canadians regarded the American move to lure athletes across the border for pay as an attack on their national treasure. Ontario officials even threatened to banish players for selling their talents. But many stars moved anyway, including Fred Taylor, Joe Hall and Holden, who joined the Portage Lakers and scored the first goal in the very first pro-league game in December 1904. Nearly 4,000 fans witnessed Holden's historic marker against goalkeeper James MacKay in the 6–3 road win at Pittsburgh's Duquesne Gardens. The IHL only survived three seasons, but it established professional hockey in North America. The game would never be the same.

Sidney Crosby, Pittsburgh Penguins, January 1, 2008

Falling snow, a jubilant crowd, a close game and a rising star in the spotlight—the 2008 Winter Classic unfolded just as if the NHL had scripted it. Played outdoors at Buffalo's Ralph Wilson Stadium in front of an NHL-record 71,217 fans, the contest was billed as a return to the roots of hockey. In a nod to nostalgia, both teams wore throwback uniforms. The Buffalo Sabres were outfitted in the white, blue and gold jerseys they last used during the 1995–96 season, while the Pittsburgh Penguins donned powder blue and black uniforms from the early 1970s. Many players wore hats to guard against the cold, including Sabres goalie Ryan Miller, who wore a cap fashioned out of a hockey sock, atop his mask. The game was tied 1–1 after regulation time, and when no one scored during the five-minute overtime, it went to a shootout. After five skaters, the score stood 1–0 for Pittsburgh, setting the stage for the sixth shooter—Sidney Crosby. If the league's marquee player scored, the Penguins would win. Skating in alone beneath a violet-streaked sky with snowflakes blowing in his face, Crosby eluded a poke-check by Miller and stuffed a shot between the goalie's pads. "Me with the last shot—I think I did that a lot of times, when I was young," Crosby said afterwards, summing up a perfect end to a perfect day.

PICTURE CREDITS

INDEX

ACKNOWLEDGEMENTS

Thanks to the following organizations for use of quoted and/or statistical material:

· *The Hockey News.* Reprinted by permission of *The Hockey News*, a division of Transcontinental Inc.

· *The Official NHL Guide and Record Book,* various editions. Published by Total Sports Canada, including 2010.

· *Total Hockey Second Edition, Total Stanley Cup* © 1998, 2000 and *Total NHL,* © 2003 by Dan Diamond and Associates Inc. Published by Total Sports, 1998, 2000, 2003.

· The Associated Press; *Boston Herald*; Canadian Press; *Detroit News*; *Edmonton Journal*; ESPN; *Elias Sports Bureau*; *Globe and Mail*; *Hockey Night in Canada*; *Montreal Gazette*; *Montreal Herald*; *Montreal Star*; *National Post*; *New York Times*; *Ottawa Citizen*; *Pittsburgh Press*; *Toronto Star*; and *Sports Illustrated*.

Numerous other books and publications corroborated our research, including *Canada on Ice* by Dave Holland; *Century of Hockey* by Steve Dryden; *Cold War* by Roy MacSkimming; *The Days Canada Stood Still* by Scott Morrison; *Etched in Ice* by Michael McKinley; *Go to the Net* by Al Strachan; *Gretzky to Lemieux* by Ed Willes; *The Last Hurray* by Stephen Cole; *100 Great Moments in Hockey* by Brian Kendall; 629

by 9 by I. Sheldon Posen; *Sixty Moments that Changed the Game* by Jason Kay; *The Trail of the Stanley Cup* by Charles L. Coleman; and *World of Hockey* by Szymon Szemberg and Andrew Podnieks.

Also helpful in our research were video-sharing websites such as YouTube; Internet databases such as the Hockey Summary Project at hsp.flyershistory.net, hockeyDB.com, iihf.com, nhl.com, espn.com, hhof.com, and shrpsports.com.

The authors gratefully acknowledge all the help from Benny Ercolani of the NHL; Craig Campbell at the Hockey Hall of Fame; Society for International Hockey Research; Seth Martin and Bobby Kromm; photographer Thomas Konigsthal Jr.; Sheldon Posen at the Canadian Museum of Civilization; Boston Public Library; McLellan Library at McGill University; Rob Sanders and Susan Rana at Greystone Books; designers Peter Cocking and Jessica Sullivan; the many hockey writers and broadcast and web journalists who have made the game better through their own work; and editor Derek Fairbridge.

DON WEEKES is a producer at CTV Montreal.
He has written numerous hockey trivia and
statistical books, including *The Biggest Book of
Hockey Trivia*, and co-authored *Hockey's Top
100: The Game's Greatest Records*.

KERRY BANKS is an award-winning magazine
writer and author. He has published 17 books
on sports and resides in Vancouver.